OPEN AND DISTANCE LEARNING SERIES

Open and Flexible Learning in Vocational Education and Training

JUDITH CALDER & ANN McCOLLUM

**KOGAN
PAGE**

YOURS TO HAVE AND TO HOLD

BUT NOT TO COPY

First published in 1998

Apart from any fair dealing for the purposes of research or private study, or criticism or review, as permitted under the Copyright, Designs and Patents Act 1988, this publication may only be reproduced, stored or transmitted, in any form or by any means, with the prior permission in writing of the publishers, or in the case of reprographic reproduction, in accordance with the terms and licences issued by the Copyright Licensing Agency. Enquiries concerning reproduction outside those terms should be sent to the publishers at the undermentioned address:

Kogan Page Limited
120 Pentonville Road
London N1 9JN

© Judith Calder and Ann McCollum 1998

The right of Judith Calder and Ann McCollum to be identified as the authors of this work has been asserted by them in accordance with the Copyright, Designs and Patents Act 1988.

British Library Cataloguing in Publication Data

A CIP record for this book is available from the British Library.

ISBN 0 7494 2172 X

Typeset by Kogan Page
Printed and bound in Great Britain by Clays Ltd, St Ives plc

Open and Flexible Learning in Vocational Education and Training

Open and Distance Learning Series

Series Editor: Fred Lockwood

Activities in Self-Instructional Texts, Fred Lockwood
Becoming an Effective Open and Distance Learner, Perc Marland
Exploring Open and Distance Learning, Derek Rowntree
Improving Your Students' Learning, Alistair Morgan
Key Terms and Issues in Open and Distance Learning, Barbara Hodgson
Making Materials-Based Learning Work, Derek Rowntree
Managing Open Systems, Richard Freeman
Mega-Universities and Knowledge Media, John S Daniel
Objectives, Competencies and Learning Outcomes, Reginald F Melton
Open and Distance Learning: Case Studies from Education, Industry and Commerce,
    Stephen Brown
Open and Flexible Learning in Vocational Education and Training, Judith Calder and
    Ann McCollum
Preparing Materials for Open, Distance and Flexible Learning, Derek Rowntree
Programme Evaluation and Quality, Judith Calder
Teaching Through Projects, Jane Henry
Teaching with Audio in Open and Distance Learning, Greville Rumble
The Costs and Economics of Open and Distance Learning, Greville Rumble
Understanding Learners in Open and Distance Education, Terry Evans
Using Communications Media in Open and Flexible Learning, Robin Mason

Contents

Series editor's foreword vii
Preface ix

1. **The looming crisis** 1
   Background 1
   Education, training and the economy 2
   The vocational education and training crisis 5
   The shift towards open, flexible and distance methods 7
   Extent of participation 14

2. **The major stakeholders** 19
   Major players in the field of open and distance learning 19
   Changes in power between stakeholder groups 23
   Changes within stakeholder groups 27

3. **What problem is being solved?** 40
   Human capital 40
   Employers' problems 43
   Learners' aims 50
   The training providers 54
   Discussion 57

4. **Open, flexible and distance options** 60
   Introduction 60
   Perceptions of OFL provision 60
   Key design features in open and flexible courses 62
   Access and participation 63
   Study setting 65
   Curriculum 66
   Media 67
   Support 69
   Pacing and duration 74
   Assessment 75
   Putting the pieces together 77

5. **The effectiveness of open and flexible approaches**   **86**
    Introduction   86
    What stakeholders mean by effectiveness   87
    How do we measure learning effectiveness?   92
    Achieving effective learning   98

6. **Selecting and implementing appropriate solutions**   **106**
    Introduction   106
    Key factors determining the selection of training programmes 107
    The training challenge   110
    Critical issues arising in the implementation of open learning 116
    programmes
    Common themes and concerns   120

7. **Critical issues**   **123**
    Introduction   123
    Who do we mean when we talk of employers?   124
    Workforce attitudes   127
    Front-line training providers   129
    Whose needs is the government meeting?   130
    Conclusion   131

References   **135**

Index   **141**

Series editor's foreword

In his book, *Technology, Open Learning and Distance Education*, Tony Bates predicted, from Canadian data, that 'Someone leaving school today will need to be retrained at least five times in their working life'. He went on to say

> ... if every worker currently in the work force was sent back to college for three months training every five years (a very conservative estimate for the average amount of job-based training required), the post-secondary education system in Canada, already one of the most comprehensive in the world, would have to increase by more than 50 per cent. Even if tax payers were willing to create more colleges and universities, this would be an inappropriate response for most of this target group, who are working, have families, and cannot afford or do not want to be full-time students.

These claims and observations are not restricted to Canada or to other developed countries – they are applicable worldwide. We are all increasingly aware that capital, and jobs, flow to where competent labour is cheapest and that the need to increase, let alone sustain the quality of the labour force, is a major factor in the economic future of industry and commerce; and to the viability of social services. Many of us are also aware of the cost of training and the difficulties in assessing its effectiveness.

It is in this context that this book is so timely. The book emerged from a study designed to compare the learning effectiveness of open and flexible learning methods with traditional methods in vocational education and training; a thorny problem which raised a whole series of issues that anyone involved in vocational educational and training, or open, flexible and distance education, will find of value.

The initial discussion of 'the looming crisis' is initially sobering but then encouraging – it reinforces the point that Tony Bates raised several years ago. It is sobering, in that until recently only small proportions of UK employees had received recent training and educational opportunities, small proportions of UK companies had any training plans and many had no budget; a training environment that did not compare favourably with our international competitors. However, evidence assembled by Judith Calder and Ann McCollum reveal that in a relatively short period large proportions of companies are employing open, distance and flexible training methods to increase access and participation and to provide flexible provision. Furthermore, a whole series of training initiatives, including the University for Industry, are under discussion.

A major feature of the book, besides the unpacking of the numerous and interconnected issues associated with the use of open, distance and flexible training methods in vocational education and training, is the use of actual illustrations drawn from a variety of companies – large and small. Judith and Ann illustrate the relationship between the stakeholders involved, their differing perceptions and their training needs. They discuss the strengths and weaknesses of various approaches and the effectiveness of learning as well as the challenges and opportunities that surround us.

If you are involved in vocational educational and training and either employing open, flexible and distance methods, or thinking of doing so, this book is required reading. It will undoubtedly challenge some of your assumptions, encourage you to consider your current practices and provide valuable insights for the benefit of everyone.

Fred Lockwood

Preface

Over the last 25 years there has been a phenomenal growth worldwide in the development and use of open, flexible and distance approaches for learning. An increasingly diverse range of delivery mechanisms is now being used to enable people, wherever they are – in remote villages, on the high seas, in factories, shops and offices, at home with children – to take advantage of an ever-growing variety of learning opportunities. This phenomenon has been observed by, and in many cases, enthusiastically supported and encouraged by government. In the UK, Government bodies such as the former Manpower Services Commission, subsequently the Employment Department and then the Department for Education and Employment, have played a key role in supporting and promoting the principles of open, flexible and distance learning in the field of vocational education and training.

This book is intended for policy makers, managers, practitioners, and all those involved in vocational education and training, as well as open and distance education specialists interested in the particular issues raised by the application of these methodologies to vocational education and training. It has emerged from the research undertaken for a study commissioned by the Department for Education and Employment in 1994. The focus of that work was on the learning effectiveness of open and flexible learning when used for vocational education as compared with traditional vocational education courses (Calder *et al.*, 1995, McCollum and Calder, 1995). The concerns of this book are somewhat wider, in that we have considered the role of the broader context and in particular the concerns of the different groups of stakeholders in determining the direction of developments in vocational education and the contribution which open, flexible and distance approaches can make. The three themes we consider then are the environment in which education and training strategy is determined and delivered; the nature of the major stakeholders and of the needs being addressed; and the resulting behaviours – the types of provision made available, the implementation of training provision and the different outcomes which result.

At the time we undertook the original study, the concern of the then Employment Department was that while considerable attention had been paid to the cost-effectiveness of open and flexible learning, the question of its learning effectiveness had attracted rather less attention. The study which ensued involved searching through the international and national literature to review existing evidence about the learning effectiveness of open and flexible learning, and designing the research so that different types of learning in both the public sector and industrial and commercial sectors were included.

The research was designed as an in-depth study of providers of vocational education and training offering basic level courses both in traditional form and as open and flexible courses. The challenges encountered in the selection of the sample for the study provided a foretaste of the problems which face most researchers in this area. Public providers advertise their courses in a range of publications and their courses are listed, with varying degrees of accuracy, on a number of databases. However, there is no listing of companies which provide in-company training for their employees. It is possible to construct lists of companies with an interest in open and distance training by getting together lists of advertisers, participants at conferences and training workshops and the like, but such lists are inevitably limited and biased. We used lists from three different sources to construct a basic sampling frame of companies with a known interest in open and distance provision, and undertook phone interviews with them as a preliminary sift to find companies actually providing both traditional courses and open and flexible courses to basic and craft level staff. As we reported at the time:

> We encountered a number of problems at this stage stemming from the fact that most of the organizations were undergoing major reorganisations of their training and development programmes. With training programmes in such a state of transition and uncertainty, and with reorganisation signifying re-trenchment in many cases, the project was seen to touch upon a politically sensitive area. Given these circumstances, it generally took a number of weeks for managers to give the project due consideration and to decide whether or not it was feasible for them to partake in the study. The fact that training currently has such a high profile within companies is both fortunate and unfortunate, for although it does make this a very interesting period in which to look at company training, it did mean that a number of companies which might otherwise have taken part subsequently felt unable to do so (Calder *et al.*, 1995).

We selected a purposive sample of 42 different courses from eight different public providers and in-company training schemes. The aim was to select courses covering a range of different skills: interpersonal, cognitive and motor. Phone interviews were carried out with a range of providers of training and education who used both open, distance and flexible approaches and traditional approaches. There were interviews and discussions with 58 training managers, tutors and trainers. We also asked 505 trainees and students to complete various self-completion questionnaires and inventories.

The use of self-completion questionnaires and a learning inventory presented some challenges as they had to be suitable for completion by people with greatly varying degrees of maturity and literacy. The aim was for members of the research team to personally administer and collect the questionnaires from the trainees and students. Where this was not possible, they were administered either by the tutor for the course, or sent direct by post to the student. In studying training provision, we wanted to consider environmental influences, organizational factors, course-specific variables and student demographics and learning styles. The inventory which we eventually decided to use was Entwistle and Tait's 'Approaches to Study' inventory which has been widely used in the UK, although primarily with students in higher education.

Over the period since the fieldwork was completed, we have presented and discussed the findings at a number of national workshops and international conferences. Reports from the study, and the papers we have presented, have enabled us to get a range of feedback on the findings. However, the scope of this book means that we have also drawn widely on the thinking and research of many others and we acknowledge our debt to them.

For many years now, basic level vocational education and training has been very much the poor relation when it came to either funding or status. While higher education in the UK has had a long history of developing and offering applied vocational courses for the élite at undergraduate and graduate levels, its record at sub-degree level has been, to say the least, unimpressive. The University for Industry is being promoted as the solution which will achieve for vocational education and training what the Open University has achieved for open participation in higher education in the UK. To what extent it will be successful remains to be seen.

There are some signs that the climate for vocational education may be changing. The publication of the Green Paper on lifelong learning in February 1998 laid out the UK Government's plans for and commitments to the development of lifelong learning in England (DfEE 1998). Further proposals for Scotland and Wales are expected, together with papers on the University for Industry, Individual Learning Accounts and National Targets. However while the need to widen participation in and access to learning is one of the key principles highlighted in the Green Paper, there are widespread concerns about the funding levels and funding mechanisms which will accompany new developments. As Edwards *et al.*, (1998) point out:

> Local conditions and the opportunity structures within them impact significantly on the learning trajectories of different groups, suggesting a need for the regionalization and localization of policies to support lifelong learning. There are concerns that a learning society, which primarily sustains a learning market will have the effect of marginalizing issues of non-participation and social exclusion.

The book introduces theory as well as research and practice. Kurt Lewin is credited with the aphorism that 'There is nothing so practical as a good theory'. The purpose of theory is to provide the underpinning explanation for sets of seemingly diverse, but interlinked events. Two rather different kinds of outcome can then result. One is where understanding and hence prediction is improved; while the other is where people are thereby helped to make events come about – what Argyris and Schön call 'theories of action'. Theories of action do lead to understanding and prediction, but then go beyond these relatively passive outcomes by providing people with a base from which they can take action (Argyris and Schön, 1978).

Chapter 1 introduces the background against which developments in the use of open, flexible and distance approaches to vocational education and training need to be seen and interpreted. The economic and political forces which have led to the decision to expand provision and participation in training, the shifting boundaries of responsibility and the tensions which have accompanied the displacement of traditional practices by more radical ones are all introduced.

We then move on to a consideration of the major stakeholders in the field of open, flexible and distance learning and vocational education and training. The core stakeholders are identified as government, employers, training providers and trainees. However, the list is increasing as new interest groups are drawn in through the use of new and innovative approaches to vocational education and training. We point out that it is necessary to use a stakeholder approach if the effects of the often conflicting aims, interests, and criteria of success of the different interest groups are to be adequately taken account of. We are not dealing with a static situation, however, and the changes in power between stakeholder groups over the past few years, and, as importantly, the changes within different stakeholder groups are described and discussed.

Vocational education and training may be seen as a solution to certain societal economic and social problems at the one level, or to the successful operation of businesses or to the achievement of a rewarding and satisfying working life at another. However, the needs of stakeholders between these different levels may conflict or coincide. Chapter 3 examines the educational, training and learning needs which vocational education and training is expected to meet, and the constraints within which training solutions have to be found. The concept of human capital is introduced in order to clarify and highlight the distinction between the skills and knowledge which are transferable between jobs, and those which can only be productively used by the worker's current employer.

While tutors in different settings feel quite comfortable with such terms as 'open', 'flexible' and 'distance', their understanding of the terms does reflect the particular settings within which they have to work. In Chapter 4, we move on to looking at actual examples of open, flexible and distance learning solutions to training problems. The variety of solutions to different vocational education and training problems do reflect these different perceptions. We examine the range of key design features which go together to make up a course: access, study settings, teaching media, support, pacing and assessment. We also examine the strengths and weaknesses of the different ways in which these features are put together in our case study examples.

In Chapter 5 the effectiveness of student learning through open, flexible and distance methods is examined. The cost savings and the increased participation and access opportunities offered through these methods have been well researched and reported. The opportunities offered for minimizing disruptions to work and of introducing choice into the timing, pace and duration of training are becoming increasingly recognized. However, for many in the field, there are questions remaining about the types of skill and knowledge which can be effectively taught by other than tried and tested traditional means. Similarly, assumptions continue to be made about the types of student who can cope with what are seen by many as the more challenging methods of open, flexible and distance learning. Learning theory, however, does suggest that the factors which are likely to play a role in the effectiveness of learning are more likely to lie in other directions. The work of leading thinkers and researchers into the different ways in which people learn – their learning styles and the strategies they use – are introduced, and the findings about the learning styles found among the trainees on our study are discussed.

This leads on to the questions which training providers have to address when selecting training programmes. Chapter 6 examines the problems faced by providers who are charged with the responsibility for matching training needs against training options. The four key areas of concern are seen as the overall purpose of the training, the educational goals, the context of the employing organization and the particular target population for the training programme. These concerns are set against the selection of the training options, with examples of different delivery methods discussed in terms of their appropriateness for the particular situation in which they were used.

The final chapter identifies the issues which we consider to present both the greatest challenges and the greatest opportunities for those connected with vocational education and training. While open, flexible and distance solutions are seen as powerful tools, the use of which has stimulated creative and imaginative solutions to many training problems, there remain a number of key critical issues for vocational education and training, which remain to be addressed. The extent to which there may be a connection between the lack of appropriately skilled workers and the lack of training provision for staff at the bottom of the ladder – craft grade and basic operative staff – is referred to. At the same time the tendency to talk about 'employers' as a homogeneous group is clearly unhelpful when they range from the immense number of one- and two-person businesses to global companies employing tens of thousands of people and controlling greater amounts of wealth than do many countries. We discuss the differences between large, medium and small enterprises in terms of their training provision and their attitudes to training. At the same time, the relationship between workforce attitudes and current employment practices is discussed and in particular, the need for the careful planning and sensitive introduction of new training schemes. The issue of the front-line training providers is also highlighted. Cost-led changes have left many trainers in both the public and private sectors feeling exposed and vulnerable and the need for acknowledging the problems this causes at a time when radical changes in trainers' roles are needed is discussed.

This final chapter concludes by discussing the relevance of contingency theory for individual providers and users of vocational education and training. The reality is that there is no simple answer to the range of needs to which the different stakeholders are seeking solutions. However, there are optimal solutions for individual-providing organizations and for individual businesses. It is clear that open, flexible and distance approaches to training offer us a set of powerful tools which challenge current thinking on education and training. There is still a long way to go as we explore the potential of new approaches for different types of learners and for the acquisition of different types of skills and knowledge. The extent to which we make the most of these tools will depend to a large extent on the degree to which the political environment changes, so that both trainers and trainees lose their fear of the personal economic consequences of change, and come to see training as an opportunity for personal development and achievement rather than as the agent of further failure.

Chapter 1

The looming crisis

Background

A general consensus is emerging that there has been a major growth in the use of open, flexible and distance methods for vocational education and training. Alternative forms of education and training provision are increasingly being seen as more effective than traditional forms in meeting the specific education and training needs of a wide range of people. This growth has been driven by an underlying and growing concern regarding the accessibility, and the provision of practical vocational education and training, which is relevant to the needs of employers and the national economy. It is claimed that 70 per cent of companies are now engaged in some form of open learning and furthermore that open learning is now embedded in the workplace.

> ... open and distance learning has become embedded in the workplace, with larger companies establishing open learning centres which have in some cases expanded opportunity beyond the company's immediate needs on the grounds that a learning organization represents a company objective whatever the area of training (Tait, 1992).

In order to understand how and why this has come about, it is necessary to identify the fundamental shifts that have taken place within vocational education and training. These shifts have taken place not only within the UK but also on a worldwide basis and have prompted industry and governments alike to invest in the development of open and distance learning programmes. The opening chapter explores the importance of open, flexible and distance education to vocational education and training.

Firstly, the key economic and political forces underlying the shifts, which have taken place in vocational education and training, are examined; in particular the critical issues at the heart of vocational education and training such as the need to provide relevant workplace-based training, the need to expand provision and participation and the need for a flexible workforce. The chapter then moves on to consider the crisis in vocational education and training and the pressure to adopt radical measures such as open, flexible and distance approaches to training provision. It is concluded by considering the shifting boundaries in relation to training providers and training sites, the switch in focus on to the learner and learning outcomes and the critical tensions, which are accompanying the displacement of traditional approaches by open, flexible and distance methods.

Education, training and the economy

Globalization

The expansion of vocational education and training in the UK represents the attempts by government and industry to respond to the profound changes that have taken place in the global economy. The market-driven nature of current globalization has fed upon 'the growth of world trade, the emergence of internationalized knowledge systems, the changing patterns of communication, the penetration of technology into the social fabric of communities, production, consumption and the promotion of internationalism as a cultural value' (Dhanarajan, 1997). As the president of the Commonwealth of Learning pointed out in a major speech in Kuala Lumpur in November 1997, deregulation has reduced national governments' control over the movement and value of currency and control over foreign investments while globalizing competition among workforces. Capital now flows to wherever competent labour is cheapest and least subject to regulation. As he concluded 'The result is reflected in the greater vocationalisation of our education systems and, more importantly, puts pressure on the system to provide retraining for those whose jobs are lost and to develop training programmes in communities where jobs move into' (Dhanarajan, 1997).

Similar points have also been made by other authorities. Capitalism is again revolutionizing the instruments of production, as Forrester et al., 1995 state 'there has been a major shift in the spatial organization of capital... (and) a qualitative shift in production methods in the advanced industrial countries'. These shifts are characterized by post-Fordist principles of 'diversity, differentiation and fragmentation' and as technology, production systems and organizational structures have become more complicated, so there has been a parallel increase in the need to augment experiences of education and work (Tuijnman, 1992). Thus, as Edwards (1991) argues, the post-Fordist shifts in the economy are paralleled by similar shifts in education and training. An Australian Report (National Board of Employment, 1992) is cited by Edwards as identifying the typical pressures and constraints which have led to these shifts:

the pressure of increasing students numbers; the unmet demands for new buildings; a 'shortage' of academic staff (or, more likely, academic posts!); and the pressures to serve industry, to become more entrepreneurial and to export education. These factors are echoed elsewhere around the globe, resulting in a general shift towards technologically mediated and flexible forms of delivery to the extent where it is possible to argue that 'the boundary between "distance education" and "conventional education" is likely to disappear'... (Edwards, 1997).

The expansion of vocational education and training has thus been accompanied by qualitative shifts in its nature. A key theme in the debates on vocational education and training revolves around the need for a workforce that can cope with the changing demands of the international economic environment. A country's workforce is seen as a critical success factor in its international competitiveness, and vocational education and training is seen as crucial in the development of a multi-skilled workforce.

Western European trends in training provision

In a review of adult education and training in Europe, Tuijnman draws on a range of studies carried out throughout Europe to identify general trends in European training, and while he states that countries are moving in different directions, the one common trend he identifies is the marked quantitative growth in vocational education and training. Thus, the concerns of governments and employers alike about vocational training have been reflected by an increased investment in this area. A number of European studies have argued that economic success depends on having a competitive 'high-tech' industry, and that previous under-investment in vocational education and training have undermined European efforts to respond to changing economic conditions, thus most European countries are now placing a 'heavy emphasis on policies to improve job training' (Tuijnman, 1992).

Over the past decades, the UK government's approach to vocational education and training has been distinctive from most other European countries in one key respect, namely that individual employers take primary responsibility for training their employees. It is they who choose how much (and whether) to invest in training. Thus, while many other European countries provide legislative backing to training, the UK has had no mechanisms to ensure minimum standards or levels of provision in training. Until the change in Government policy announced in December 1997, in which employers are obliged to offer young workers a day a week paid leave for study, companies chose whether or not to opt in to government training initiatives and standards such as NVQs, the Investors in People Initiative and the National Education and Training Targets (NETTs). As Forrester *et al.* (1995) observed (Example 1.1):

The small number of employers involved in the new training system are often self-selected enthusiasts and are in no way representative of most British companies, and in particular, of small and medium sized enterprises.

Governments in countries such as France and Germany have taken a strong role in creating training structures and providing legislative back-up. France for example has provided individual rights to training leave, and has a remissible training levy on all employers. In Germany there is compulsory employer membership of training bodies (Keep, 1993)(Example 1.1). The UK Government, however, persisted with voluntarist training schemes despite calls from major employers and bodies such as the Institute of Directors for government legislation which establishes compulsory minimum standards of training (Keep, 1993)(Example 1.1).

Example 1.1: Western European trends in training provision

- In 1991 the National Institute of Adult and Continuing Education stated that 70 per cent of employees had had no recent training or education opportunities at work (Forrester *et al.*, 1995).
- In 1991 an Employment Department report 'Skills needs in Britain' found that 29 per cent of British companies have no training plan and 34 per cent have no training budget (Forrester *et al.*, 1995).
- In Germany, about 67 per cent of all workers possess vocational qualifications; in the UK the figure is about 36 per cent (Keep, 1993).

In comparison with other European countries then, vocational education and training in Britain is very poor in terms of levels of provision and participation in training and also in terms of the organization and management of training.

While many argue that the perceived link between the economy and education and training is both overstated and simplistic, nevertheless, this view has gained such currency in the UK that it has largely circumscribed the discourse, the direction and the development of vocational education in the 1990s. For example, the need for both quantitative and qualitative changes in vocational training has been expressed by the House of Lords Select Committee on training, the House of Commons Trade and Industry Committee, the Confederation of British Industry and the National Institute of Adult and Continuing Education (Forrester *et al.*, 1995). However, the extent to which a government can rely on education and training to deliver growth should be questioned. Others point out that while the view that inadequate vocational education has been a major factor in Britain's poor economic performance has become widely accepted, it has not necessarily been proven (Forrester *et al.*, 1995). What is quite clear, however, is that the acceptance of this view has had a profound impact upon the nature of vocational education and training in the UK. As Esland states (Forrester *et al.*, 1995):

> The displacement of responsibility for economic failure and decline from the political and economic arenas to the educational and training institutions...

has had the effect of distorting public policy debate about the relationship between economic change, education and employment... It has also provided legitimation of the imposition of a market forces model on the education provided by schools and colleges.

The changing employment context, characterized by post-Fordist patterns of production and organization requires new working methods, and the key features repeatedly identified of the ideal 1990s' workforce are flexibility, adaptability and multiple skills (Forrester *et al.*, 1995). The learning requirements of the workforce revolve around the need for continuous training in a wider range of skills which serve to increase 'the adaptability of the employee to changing production methods' (Forrester *et al.*, 1995).

The vocational education and training crisis

The UK Government response to the perceived crisis in vocational training has been characterized by three key interlocking features:

- firstly, the marketplace is viewed as the key instrument in the delivery of appropriate training
- secondly, the government has taken further steps to devolve responsibility for training to employers and employees
- lastly, given the emphasis on the labour force as a key factor in economic success, training is increasingly being viewed in highly instrumental terms.

Because public education is seen as having failed to provide appropriate education and training which meets employers' needs, there has been a shift towards work-based learning. In order to redress the mismatch between adult education provision and the education and training needs of the workforce, employers have been urged to take primary responsibility for funding and directly providing training. Thus, the workplace itself has become the site of learning, and rather than the government legislating to ensure that training does take place, the marketplace is viewed as the central means by which to ensure training needs will be met:

> The basic idea is that the matching of demand and supply of adult education and training should be left to the play of market forces (Tuijnman, 1992).

Thus, the government sought to substantially expand vocational education and training without incurring additional expenditure which would instead be borne by employers and individuals. As the Government White Paper for Employment for the 1990s so clearly states:

> employers as both providers and consumers of training have the primary responsibility for ensuring that our labour force has the skills to support an expanding economy (cited in Forrester *et al.*, 1995).

The TUC questions whether individual investment decisions can provide the trained workforce that the economy needs (Tuckett, 1991). This concern is strongly reinforced by the European Free Trade Association (EFTA), which is highly critical of single employer financing of training, both because it tends to result in a narrow form of job-specific training, and also in training opportunities which tend to be restricted to a small proportion of the workforce (Forrester *et al.*, 1995). While the government has developed national systems of qualifications (NVQs) and national standards and targets for training (NETTs), in practice levels of training provision vary widely and the quality and quantity of training programmes within various companies and sectors are far from standardized. The nature and extent of training opportunities available in companies are solely dependent upon the individual employer's attitudes to training. Thus, while some major companies such as Ford and Rover offer examples of attempts to broaden training efforts and 'emphasise the motivational benefits of training for all levels of the workforce at all stages of their working lives' (Keep, 1993), the overall consensus is that British companies are failing to invest adequately in vocational education and training. However, there is some compelling evidence that companies have not only begun to invest more in training, but also that the status of training is rising, with training now playing a central role in company development (Saggers, 1994). As shown in Example 1.2 a training survey was carried out in 1994, which included the following findings:

Example 1.2: A new wave of training

- 68 per cent of companies had increased levels of training in the previous two years
- 58 per cent of firms had a board member with defined responsibility for training
- 61 per cent said training had been instigated to improve quality
- 59 per cent said restructuring was the catalyst for training
- 65 per cent said they had increased the level of line manager involvement in training.

Source: Saggers (1994)

One of the stated aims in the recent developments in vocational education and training has been to expand the provision of and participation in training, and to enhance the accessibility and flexibility of training. However, many recent studies argue that the limited opportunities available for vocational education and training actually serve to marginalize the majority of the workforce who have either limited or no access. For example, Edwards argues that in the future 25 per cent of the workforce will have job security and training, while the other 75 per cent will suffer from job insecurity and will have limited training opportunities (Edwards *et al.*, 1993). Thus, there will be a 'core' of highly skilled, highly educated workers while the majority of the workforce is consigned to the 'periphery' of low skill, low pay, low-security work with training, which can actually serve 'to inhibit job flexibility and inhibit the possibilities of progression' (Forrester *et al.*, 1995).

While such a scenario is hypothetical, there is some evidence to support this view of training trends. For example, in the 1994 survey of training referred to above, it was also found that 58 per cent of companies had expanded management training, and 52 per cent had expanded supervisory training, in marked contrast to the training of operatives, which was increased by only 32 per cent of firms and training of sales staff which had only been increased by 25 per cent of firms. Thus, as Saggers (1994) observes, 'Increases in delivery at these more senior levels far exceeded growth in any other area'.

This serves to highlight the need to ask critical questions in relation to developments in vocational education and training, which cuts through the rhetoric of participation and flexibility by explicitly recognizing the distinctive interests of three key sets of stakeholders in education and training; namely the government, employers and employees. In contrast to the bleak scenario outlined by Edwards, the example of 'joint programmes' in North America which Ferman discusses highlights an alternative model of training provision which represents an opportunity 'to address simultaneously management concerns with competitiveness and flexibility, labour concerns with employment security and career opportunities, and government concerns with human resource capabilities' (Forrester *et al.*, 1995).

While a general consensus has been reached regarding the need for new and expanded forms of vocational education and training, there are underlying tensions in relation to the short- and long-term goals of education, between an instrumental and a more comprehensive approach to training, and between the different stakeholder interests in education. These tensions will come to the fore in the choices that are to be made regarding the implementation of open learning programmes, as Robinson argues:

> The growth of open learning in the context of vocational education has highlighted the tension between open access and open pedagogy... The aims of the (Open Tech) Programme were explicitly concerned with providing the workforce with industrially useful competencies rather than competencies related to life in more general terms... Access was a central issue because it was acknowledged that the workforce needed to be trained as it worked and so the open access aspects were seized as an essential part of the process (Robinson 1989).

The shift towards open, flexible and distance methods

The call upon companies to adapt to shifts in the economy by enhancing workforce skills and, therefore, also to provide the necessary training to produce a multi-skilled workforce stem back to the early 1980s as the MSC statement below clearly illustrates (Magee and Alexander, 1986):

The need is urgent:

- to raise the productivity and improve the flexibility and motivation of the labour force
- to enable management and other employees to adjust quickly and effectively to new methods, processes, products, services and technologies
- to overcome skills shortages which may develop and impede growth or innovation, and ensure that there is sufficient training in emerging new skill
- to enable individuals to update and extend their skills, often on a quite radical basis, and to develop throughout their lives.

However, it was only in the 1990s that a broad range of companies finally accepted the challenge, and began to recognize the central role that training can play within an organization, as Saggers' 1994 survey shows:

In this shift, organizations are having to become far more flexible in order that learners have access to opportunities relevant to their needs, when, where and how they want them. The transmission of learning... is in the process of being replaced by individual learning programmes tied to the needs of particular individuals, mixing elements of formal, non-formal and informal learning.

Recent research suggests that over 75 per cent of companies are actively involved in training (Crequer, 1997b). However, this appears to be true only of medium and larger companies (ie those with over 100 employees). The reality is that the smaller the company, the less likely it is that any open learning opportunities will be available to the employees. So, for example, a national survey carried out by the NOP for the Department of Employment found that at that time, only about 10 per cent of establishments saw themselves as making use of open learning in their training, although among larger establishments (100 plus employees) usage was reported at around 34 per cent. How open and distance learning is perceived is clearly crucial when it comes to matters of estimating penetration. NOP reported that by using definitions which specified the individual media which could be used in open learning, 52 per cent of companies said that they had used open learning at some point (National Opinion Polls, 1992).

Gathering accurate data on the levels of open learning provision within UK companies is remarkably difficult, as Pell tells us:

The amount and quality of information available in the UK is simply not as high as is the case in many of our European competitors... Reliance has thus to be placed on snapshot views of employer activity gathered through surveys. These have in themselves revealed the paucity of British employer' attempts to create and maintain detailed records of levels of training activities and expenditure (Pell, cited in Keep, 1990).

A key problem in the literature on in-company vocational training, especially in relation to new trends in training such as the movement towards open learning, is that much of the literature focuses on a limited number of major international companies, which represent a small section of companies in the UK. For example, companies such as Ford, Rover, and Nissan UK are among a handful of companies whose practices are referred to repeatedly in discussions on training (Keep, 1993, Forrester *et al.*, 1995). However, such companies represent the exception rather than the rule. Thus, while they are highly significant in terms of highlighting one of the possible directions in training, they tend to focus on 'leading-edge' initiatives. They are, therefore, far removed from the realities and constraints that most training decision-makers face, and offer little in the nature of practical guidance or insight into workplace realities and corresponding training needs, which in practice vary widely between and within companies.

Most companies are still very new to open learning, and open learning is often seen as supplementary to other forms of learning, or is only used in some training programmes. For example, some companies use open learning as a prerequisite for their traditional workshops; others integrate open and traditional modes into courses, and others are moving over completely to open learning.

Clearly then, the rhetoric surrounding the great expansion of open learning is unhelpful and misleading. In the research we undertook into company training, the difficulties encountered in identifying companies, which ran a substantial number or range of open learning programmes, is symptomatic of the fact that less open learning is taking place in companies than much of the literature would have us believe. Furthermore, given the internal diversity within organizations, the statement that a company uses open learning can be highly misleading if it implies that the whole organization is engaged in open learning, or has a uniform open learning policy, for in practice open learning is highly variable within the organizations.

The literature may be misleading for another two key reasons. Firstly, the case study format of much of the literature, whereby the most developed open learning programmes are selected for the studies, is not representative either of companies in general or, indeed, of the particular company whose high quality open learning programmes, which are highlighted in the study, are unlikely to run across the board within the company. Secondly, companies themselves will promote examples of best practice but documentation relating to problem areas, difficulties encountered in implementing training programmes or failed learning programmes will be confidential.

Another problem in relation to the literature is that many companies do not share their training experiences externally. Ireland quotes the example of a training manager at Tesco, which employs over 80 000 people, who highlights this problem:

> The fact that companies like ours spend so much time on their own training resource, working out their own competencies and generating their own training solutions means that we're a bit of a closed book (Littlefield, 1994).

Despite the limitations of current literature it does highlight a number of significant trends in relation to company training. Firstly, while the extent of open learning practice in companies may be overstated, it is nevertheless clear that increasing emphasis is being placed on the importance of training, and there is a growing interest in open and flexible forms of delivery to meet company training needs. The major qualitative shifts, which have taken place in vocational education and training, have thus stimulated a corresponding shift towards open and distance learning. Some notable trends, which will impact upon the implementation of open learning, include the following developments:

- The status of training has improved within companies.
- Training needs are more complex and many companies are moving towards tailored training programmes which, therefore, require more flexible forms of learning.
- Companies are tending to move into open learning in an attempt to integrate training into the workplace. One of the overriding purposes of adopting open learning is to provide more focused work-related training.
- There is increasing emphasis on the need to increase learning opportunities for adults and respond to learner needs.
- There has been a shift in emphasis from input models of education towards a concern with learning outcomes.

Therefore, in theory at least, there are more opportunities for learning, there are more sites of learning, and there are more methods for the delivery of learning, and the key feature underlying all of these developments is that of flexibility.

Example 1.3: Traditional training versus open learning

1. **Why traditional training fails to meet company needs:**

    - The trainers may be out of touch and lack credibility with the workforce.
    - Course content may be deemed irrelevant to the job itself.
    - Course timings may be inconvenient for the company and the workforce.
    - It can be difficult and costly to release staff from their normal duties.

2. **Benefits of open learning:**

    - Employees can learn in their own time without disrupting the organization at work or reducing productivity.
    - Employees can work at their own pace, which increases the likelihood of effective training.
    - Employees can work in private without the ignominy of classroom failure or embarrassment.

Source: Department of Employment (1990:139)

Open Learning is increasingly being identified as the key to successful training in the 1990s. For example in 1990 the *Employment Gazette* contained a special feature on open learning in which it argued that given the competitive business environment and rapid technological development, flexible approaches to training would be one of the key features of the successful organization. The article argued that traditional training frequently failed to meet company needs, for a variety of reasons (see Example 1.3).

There are diverse definitions of the terms open learning, distance education and flexible learning. Some see these terms as interchangeable while others differentiate between them. Kirkup and Jones (1996) explain some of the problems with overlapping terminology:

'Open learning' is a term recently popular in the UK and becoming more widespread, although an American educator would be more familiar with the term 'independent study'... Internationally, the term 'distance education'... is favoured over 'independent study' (Moore, 1991), especially since the use of new information and communication technologies... stresses the possibilities of communicating across distances of space and time.

Flexible learning

In a guide to flexible learning produced by the former Department of Employment (1991), they emphasize learner centred work and group work and state that flexible learning is about 'enabling the student to learn how to learn as well as learning specific subject knowledge'. The emphasis in this definition of flexible learning is therefore on the variety of skills and knowledge acquired by learners, and also the need for students to take responsibility for their own learning. The Guide (Employment, 1991) then outlines a Flexible Learning Framework which places emphasis on five key features in organizing flexible learning so that it:

- meets individual learning needs
- helps students to take on more responsibility
- makes effective use of resources
- allows for differentiated learning
- supports staff development and support.

While the need to build up what might be called a 'portfolio' of skills is also mentioned by Cooper, he lays much greater attention on the intention to meet the needs of different learners. 'Flexible learning is education and training offered in ways intended to make the provision more adaptable to the needs of different learners. A number of mechanisms, including modularization, accreditation of prior learning, open and distance learning, may be introduced by a single provider...' (Cooper, 1996). In contrast, others see flexible learning in terms of delivery systems. For example, the director of the Distance Education Centre at the University of Southern Queensland in Australia asserts that 'It is time to recognise the combined value of instructional design and flexible learning systems, which have the potential to significantly enhance staff training and development in a cost effective manner' (Taylor, 1997).

Distance education

Both Cooper and Taylor see delivery as playing a key role in flexible learning. It is, of course, the separation of teacher and learner through the use of alternative modes of delivery which makes distance education so distinctively different from traditional face-to-face provision. Thus Daniels argues that the term 'distance education' refers to those forms of instruction in which classroom sessions are not the primary means of education (Guri-Rozenblitz, 1993). While early forms of distance education relied primarily upon correspondence teaching or other single media such as radio or television, later forms used a variety of media, exploiting new technologies and advances in pedagogical thinking. Søren Nipper was the first to suggest the idea of 'generations' of distance education, based upon different delivery technologies(Nipper, 1989). He proposed that distance education could be classified into three generations:

1.   the single medium/correspondence model
2.   the multimedia model
3.   information technology/telelearning model.

A key feature of these three generations was the way in which each generation supported different teaching approaches. So, for instance, first generation distance education was characterized by very little interactivity between the student and teacher, and usually very little in the way of 'teaching' built in to the materials. Second generation distance education looked very different. As Bates (1991) points out, although the media used were still essentially one-way (print, broadcasting, cassettes), two-way communication was provided through tutors. The UK Open University is perhaps the earliest major example of this model. The development costs for second generation distance education, using a mix of specially designed and produced materials and media, meant that large numbers of students were needed to justify the costs.

It is with the third generation of distance education that most current debate is concerned. The third generation of distance education is based upon the use of electronic information technologies such as computer conferencing, audio teleconferencing, videoconferencing, and is differentiated from the first and second generation in the greater degree of interaction which they allow between the teacher and learner (Nipper 1989, Bates 1991). In America, references to distance education almost invariably refer to third generation distance education. This is in spite of the long and impressive history of institutions such as the University of Wisconsin in experimenting with and using first generation distance education methods in the early years of the twentieth century (Kirkup and Jones, 1996). However, as Bates (1991) has pointed out, the different cost structure of third generation distance education means that although production costs are much lower than for second generation distance education, the delivery costs do not bring the economies of scale achieved with second generation models.

Open learning

The common definition of open learning is learning in your own time, pace and place. The main feature emphasized here is to increase the learner's choices, and, therefore, increase accessibility. However, this is a very loose definition, which will embrace many forms of learning provision, different levels of learner choice and varying degrees of accessibility.

Carr expands upon this basic definition by telling us that the term 'open learning' describes a variety of learning arrangements, which emphasize the removal of barriers to participation and also emphasize 'the giving of greater responsibility to learners not only to determine where and when they study, but also for example what they learn, how they learn, and how they are assessed.' (Scriven, 1991). Carr draws a distinction between 'the two central concepts' in open learning, namely the opening up of access and learner-centredness, and argues that the removal of barriers in terms of place and pace in no way equates with a shift in responsibility to learners in deciding what and how they will learn; furthermore, there may be contradictions in attempting to increase access and increase learner autonomy (Carr, 1990).

Thus, distance education and open learning are not interchangeable terms, for distance education does not necessarily embrace openness in terms of pace, access or learner-centredness (see Figure 1.1). Indeed as Guri-Rozenblit (1993) states 'some distance teaching organizations should be considered as closed' (p 288).

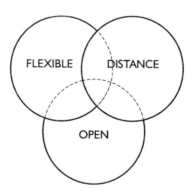

Figure 1.1 *Relationship between open, distance and flexible learning*

What is clear, both from our own research into company training practice and also from the numerous discussions about these terms, is that the term 'open' is a relative concept. Also, in relation to vocational education and training, the overall purpose of moving towards open learning or distance education is flexibility. Furthermore, the distinction between open learning and traditional learning is also blurred, given that open learning courses can contain features associated with traditional learning and vice versa. In our study of company training, for example, we found that a course described as traditional by one organization, or even one department within an organization, may be described as an open learning course by another department. We also found that perceptions of open learning varied considerably, and that people tend to relate their understanding of the terms to their own experience of provision. Thus, the term 'open learning' was applied to courses which ranged from self-contained independent learning packages (Rank Xerox), through to provision using highly structured materials, workplace-based and mentor-supervised (Safeways), to tutor-led provision using materials in support (Post Office Technical training and Inland Revenue). At the same time, the use of the term 'traditional' to describe courses, which are tutor-designed and -led, is clearly increasingly inaccurate. This is particularly the case with the workshop type tutor-led courses, which have their own sets of materials, visual aids, videos, activities and perhaps, computer-based training component. Certainly, some of the trainers with whom we talked referred to these courses as being 'open learning'.

For the purposes of this book, a very broad view of open, distance and flexible learning systems is adopted, for the central concern of the book is to consider the many different approaches using open, distance and flexible methodologies, which have been adopted within vocational education in response to the changing needs of industry. Indeed, as Summers argues, 'There are places for all the different methods; it's a question of finding the most appropriate delivery method for your particular need and organization' (Littlefield, 1994). Thus, the aim of this book is not to rate the intrinsic merits of the various forms of delivery but rather to consider which approaches are most appropriate and effective under a range of different learning needs and circumstances.

Extent of participation

There is great diversity in companies' training provision. Most companies are still very new to open learning, and open learning is often seen as supplementary to other forms of learning, or is only used in some training programmes. For example, some companies use open learning as a prerequisite for their traditional workshops; others integrate open and traditional modes into courses. Some companies are moving over completely to open learning, while others see open and traditional learning as being complementary to each other.

While there has been a growth in the use of open learning in companies, the research has failed to accurately capture the rapid developments that have taken place in current training practice. Singular case studies abound which, in failing to look at the whole picture, inevitably fail to provide any real understanding of the complex realities of providing training in a 'rapidly changing and competitive environment... in which the increasing demands for specialization compete with the need for multiskilling, flexibility and adaptability' (Scriven, 1991).

Warren provides an idealistic view of company training when he states that companies adopt a systematic approach to open learning. His view of the process of implementing open learning is that, firstly, the need for training is identified, a flexible delivery method is seen as the most effective or appropriate, consultants tender for the work and a contract is awarded, there is high commitment from management, it is, therefore, well resourced and supported within the company (Warren, 1994). However, painting such a positive view of the process of implementing open learning is not helpful to the line manager or training provider, who will face complex choices and will often have to strike a balance between conflicting practical needs and stakeholder interests when selecting learning options. As Sloman (1994) states in relation to the somewhat unrealistic view of the learning organization:

> There is, however, such a disparity between the reality of the situation that most training professionals find themselves in and the nirvana of the learning organization, that the latter may prove to be damaging and counter productive as a model for progress.

Providers

Worldwide, there are now thousands of separate providers of distance education and training. They include public and private providers; single and dual mode institutions; tiny single course providers and mega-institutions with hundreds of thousands of students. In every region of the world, in over 102 different countries, wealthy and poor, developed, newly developed and developing, open and distance provision is becoming available. The directory of Distance Learning and Supported Open Learning Worldwide includes political, religious, military and educational agencies among those organizations that offer such courses. References to in-company provision is unfortunately noticeable by its absence (ICDL, 1997b).

The number of providers in the UK of vocational education and training through open and distance methods has increased significantly since the early provision by the National Extension College and the other correspondence colleges prior to the setting up of the Open University in 1969. However, it was not until the early 1980s that open learning for vocational education and training started to move from a marginal position (Temple, 1991).

There are now three different groups of providers of training through open and distance methods:

- employers
- private providers
- public providers.

Estimates of employers using open and distance learning approaches are provided by one-off studies carried out on behalf of government departments such as the Department for Education and Employment, or for private clients such as providers of courses and materials who wish to identify marketing opportunities.

> The amount and quality of information available in the UK is simply not as high as is the case in many of our European competitors. For example, French academics can quote national statistics on the levels of retraining undertaken

in companies (Mehaut, 1988). Comparable information is simply not available here. One of the reasons for this situation is that, since the abolition of the majority of the ITBs (Industrial Training Boards) in 1981, mechanisms for gathering information on current training activity have not been available. Reliance has thus had to be placed on snapshot views of employer activity gathered through surveys. These have in themselves revealed the paucity of British employers' attempts to create and maintain detailed records of levels of training activities and expenditure (Keep, 1990: 38).

At the same time, external observers were making such comments as:

There are now few household name companies which do not use flexible learning methods of delivery as at least part of their training strategy (Warren, 1994).

It is when we turn to the number of private training providers in the UK that the scale of growth in this area can be seen. 'The broad market figures are that there are around 4,000 private training providers registered with TECS [Training and Enterprise Councils] compared with around 350 colleges' (Hoare, 1997). By no means do all these training providers use open and distance methods. Large providers of open and distance learning courses for professional and vocational purposes such as the Open University and the National Extension College are the exception. Far more typical are the units that develop specialist courses such as the Chiropody course offered by Scholl, and the Arboriculture course offered by the Horticultural Correspondence College, or other training providers who act as agents in acquiring appropriate open and distance learning courses for relatively small numbers of clients.

Example 1.4: FE College examples

1. *Hull College of FE*: open and flexible learning is provided by the college in a number of different forms. The premise is that open and flexible learning is now embedded into every curriculum area and therefore does not need any overall coordination. Open learning provision is an option on a number of different courses within most departments.

2. *Plymouth College of Further Education*: the college has been engaged in open and flexible learning since about 1984 and offers open and flexible learning in three ways:

    - flexistudy through the Flexistudy Centre
    - open learning through the Open Access Centre
    - distance education through the Open Access Centre.

The college runs along department lines whereby departments are fairly autonomous and have their own character and ways of working, and the impetus for change comes largely from within the departments themselves.

Those clients may be employers looking for a solution to a particular training need, or FE Colleges. The massive growth in the FE sector does include growth in their open and distance learning provision. However, it is here particularly that our research study suggested there were great variations in practice. Even within the same college, different departments would operate very different practices. For example, while some colleges have coordinators for their flexible learning or open learning activities, responsibility at other colleges is distributed throughout the college, lying within individual departments (Example 1.4).

Participants

If the data on actual numbers of providers engaged in open and distance education is somewhat short, then data on participants in vocational education through open and distance learning is almost non-existent. In Europe, open and distance education appears to have attracted massive numbers. A study by Keegan (1996) showed that almost 2.25 million were enrolled in distance education courses in the, then, 12 member States. 'Half were in government-organized distance training institutions: half in proprietary... *This study took no account of in-house or corporate distance training provision* (our emphases)... [nor of those]... enrolled in the European open universities and... in distance programmes from conventional universities in Europe' (Keegan, 1996).

There are some estimates of the scale of university-organized open and distance education in the US. Moore (1990) states that more than 250 000 people are enrolled in correspondence courses offered by 73 universities, and that there are 500 private home study schools. The armed forces are also major users 'of correspondence courses with the airforce alone enrolling some 400,000 persons annually' (Moore, 1990). Again, much of this provision would be for academic or professional level studies. Provision, which is more specifically vocational, is given by the figure of five million students registered with the correspondence schools who are members of the National Home Study Council. The term 'home study' is more frequently used for distance taught further education which is from technical and vocationally oriented institutions in the US (Keegan, 1996).

Broadcasting and telecommunications are increasingly seen as the main media for open and distance education and training in the US. Moore reports that major companies are increasingly using audio and video teleconferencing for in-house training programmes. As well as the National Technological University (NTU), there are generic systems and the Public Service Satellite Consortium that use satellites for their professional continuing education programmes. There are major developments using one-way video/two-way audio programmes broadcast by satellite (Moore, 1990). One of the leaders in the field, the National University Teleconferencing Network (NUTN), is a cooperative of over 250 colleges. Similarly, the National Technological University (NTU), is a collaborative venture involving 24 major US universities in producing postgraduate engineering courses. These courses are delivered by satellite to over 100 workplaces including such names as Boeing, Kodak, General Motors, IBM, Motorola and Xerox (Moore, 1990). It is clear, however, that the vast majority of the effort other than the correspondence-based programmes are directed at managerial and professional level employees, rather than at the technician and operative levels.

In the UK, both the number of providers and the number of students and trainees studying through open and distance methods has grown significantly. Again, however, accurate figures are hard to come by. Certainly the numbers of students in further education are at present rising. The 350 further education colleges provided education and training to 3.5 million students in 1995/96 – an overall increase of 16 per cent over the previous year. The vast majority of these students were part time. Annual figures for company-provided training do not exist, but special surveys suggest that in-company training is also on the increase.

> Training in all its various forms has become more common in the UK over the last 15 years. Whereas in 1984 only 8.4 per cent of employees reported having received training over a four week period, by 1992 this had risen to 13.5 per cent (see Green, Machin and Wilkinson (1996)). However, many of these courses are short-term, often only lasting a few days, and it is sensible to ask what kind of benefit to the firm and to the workers they provide. It is precisely these types of relatively short-term work-related courses – often leading to qualifications – that are the focus of our study (Blundell *et al.*, 1996).

However, these figures vary considerably between the different occupational levels, with 1 in 5 managers and other professionals reporting job-related training over a four-week period, compared to only 1 in 17 manual workers (Hillman, 1996). What proportion of this training was delivered via open and distance means is, however, unknown.

A study commissioned by the Department for Education and Employment, which was carried out in 1997, does suggest that broadening the definition of learning reveals that a higher proportion of the population than previously suspected is engaged in some learning. Over the previous three years, two-thirds, or 67 per cent of adults, had undertaken some vocational training, with about 8 per cent having undertaken self-directed learning only, rather than a taught course (Beinhart and Smith, 1998). The penetration of open, flexible and distance approaches is, as yet, difficult to identify from the analyses so far undertaken from this study. However, certain figures such as the timing of taught learning episodes being decided by only 16 per cent of learners, and that one in four recent learning episodes involved the learner 'working on his or her own from a package of materials… most commonly from written materials', do suggest that in terms of individual employees, there is as yet some considerable way to go.

Chapter 2

The major stakeholders

This chapter identifies the major stakeholders in the field of open, flexible and distance education which is used for vocational education and training. The ways in which the balance of power is changing between them, and the implications of changes within the different stakeholder groups, is analysed. The spread and adoption of new approaches to vocational education means that additional interest groups are being drawn into the field, with different sets of expectations and criteria of success. The students and trainees themselves are, of course, the key stakeholders in all this activity. A review is carried out on who the current trainees are, and identifies those who are not at present participating.

Major players in the field of open and distance learning

Why the stakeholder approach?

The history of vocational education and training through open and distance learning is one which clearly locates it as a field in which a number of different groups and agencies have a direct interest. In the corporate world, the idea of *stakeholder alliances* is gaining increasing acceptance. Management, employees and trade unions are beginning to appreciate that there might be benefits in seeing each other less as 'them' and more as 'us' or as partners, with customers and suppliers also being drawn into new alliances (Burnes, 1996). This change of heart is undoubtedly being fuelled by the fact that the longer-term investment needed for technological and organizational innovations is increasingly recognized as requiring committment to the same set of aims and objectives from all the key stakeholders (Burnes, 1996). There is increasing recognition in the literature of the distance and vocational education world of the advantages of using a stakeholder perspective in assessing developments. Examples include examining the organization and administration of distance education at degree level (Kovel-Jarvoe, 1990), and in identifying different perceptions of success in relation to the vocational education (Calder, 1993). Moore (1990) comments that:

> The key to understanding the current scene in distance education in [the United States] seems to be to recognise the collaborative, voluntary partnership between organizations representing different media, different clienteles, public and private institutions.

Given the range of key players associated with vocational education and training through open and distance learning, there are clear benefits in using the stakeholder approach in discussing the implications of research for current provision.

Core stakeholders

The groups whose interests were directly linked to mainstream vocational education using open, flexible and distance methods has not changed dramatically over the years (Example 2.1). However, their relative importance has changed as a result of new developments in technology, growing corporate interest in this field, and in some cases, because of government policies.

Example 2.1: Core stakeholders

Core vocational education and open, flexible and distance education stakeholder groups in the UK include:

- government departments
- employers
- trainees and potential trainees
- training providers – public and private sector
- local communities
- Trade unions
- accrediting agencies and awards' bodies
- publishers
- telecommunications companies
- broadcasting companies

The term 'core stakeholders' is used in the sense of those who are directly affected by policy and structures in the field and who, in turn, bring influence to bear on (Wheeler and Sillanpaa, 1997). As the list indicates, there are a considerable number of groups with a clear interest in open, flexible and distance learning developments in vocational education and training. However, the influence which each of the stakeholder groups has on policy and on strategic developments in the field is by no means equal. To a large extent this is linked to the membership of influential groups set up and given authority by the government of the day. For example, the advisory group of the UK Government's 'University for Industry' included members from higher education, further education, open and distance education, retailing, trade unions, broadcasting, film, paper manufacturing and printing and other employers (Example 2.2).

Example 2.2: Stakeholder groups represented on the membership of the government's 'University for Industry' advisory group:

- chair of the Library and Information Commission
- FE college principal
- university vice-chancellor
- chief executive of the Training and Enterprise Council's national council
- a director of Tesco
- Open University pro-vice-chancellor
- education officer of the AEEU (Associated Electrical Engineers Union)
- BBC personnel director
- chairman of Argo Wiggins
- British Film Institute director.

Source: (Nash, 1997a)

At the same time, the roles of the different stakeholder groups are not mutually exclusive. For example, employers may hold several different roles. They are 'consumers' of trained staff when they recruit skilled workers; they are training providers where they operate their own in-company training, and they are sponsors of training when they pay for external training for company workers. Similarly trade unions, as well as playing key roles in negotiating training entitlements for employed members and retraining packages for those about to be made redundant, are building upon their historical commitment to members' education by starting to provide their own open and distance courses (Spencer, 1991). Unison, for example, is currently Britain's biggest trade union. It has its own Open College which operates its own open and distance courses and training packs as well as courses through partnerships with employers and public sector providers. These are available for between 5–6000 members each year and to non-members (Hillman, 1996; ICDL, 1997b).

New stakeholders

The shift towards open and distance learning during the 1980s inevitably attracted the attention of companies who were competing with each other to adapt to and take advantage of the information age. Developments such as the co-publishing activities of the Open University in the UK attracted the attention of publishing houses and of other materials developers (Chambers, 1994). In the US, the very different direction of developments in open and distance education, focusing on electronic media, attracted the attention of telecommunications giants such as AT&T who became sponsors of the bienniel World Conference of the International Council for Distance Education in 1997. In Japan, the use of satellite and Internet technology has been promoted for distance teaching (see Case Study 2.1).

Case Study 2.1: Japan

In 1995, for example, the Ministry of Education, Science, Sport and Culture issued a report on 'practical guidelines for the New Information Age' which included models using satellite communication and fibre optic cable (Sakamoto, 1996). The establishment of a 'Space Collaboration System' (SCS) by the National Institute of Multimedia Education (NIME) in Japan comprises a hub station and 62 VSAT stations covering national universities, colleges of technology and national research institutes. As with the American NUTN, the Japanese SCS will allow these institutions to exchange and share seminars, presentations, conferences and so on using communications satellite.

In Europe there is also a clear enthusiasm for the perceived benefits of open and distance approaches to education and training as the following statement from the European Commission shows (Lewis, 1995):

> The extraordinary potential of Open Distance Learning arises from the freedom it enjoys from constraints of time, place and pace. This endows it with an extensive flexibility which makes it readily adaptable to the needs of the consumer... It can reach across the boundaries of regions, countries and continents. It has an extremely wide range of application either on its own or in conjunction with conventional education and training systems (European Commission, 1991).

By the mid-1990s, the use of telematics (telecommunications and information systems) for distance education and training was being pursued with vigour through an EC taskforce. In the same year, 1995, the EC adopted a White Paper on education and training. Edith Cresson, the European Commissioner for human resources, education, training and youth, stated that 'The Commission wishes to make Europeans aware of the profound impact caused by the information society, globalization and advances in science and technology, and the responses which education and training can make to them' (see Case Study 2.2).

Case Study 2.2: European Commission Vocational Education and Training through Open Learning Programmes

1. Telematics Applications: 20 projects have been funded under the Telematics Applications programme. They focus on training in the tourism and textile sector, hospital staff training, training of meteorology specialists, training children of migrants and publishing educational multimedia software off- and on-line.

2. Leonardo Vocational programmes: focuses on disseminating information relating to multimedia training

3. Socrates Educational programmes: focuses on the development of foreign language teaching and distance learning.

Source: Interview (1996)

In the UK, providers and potential providers of distance education and training opportunities are working with both European-funded programmes and UK Government-funded programmes as well as originating their own programmes. For example, the National Council for Educational Technology (Government-funded), the National Information and Learning Technologies (industry-funded), the Department for Education and Employment (DfEE) and the Further Education Funding Council (FEFC), are all encouraging and supporting the development of new education and training programmes which in some way utilize the new technologies.

Changes in power between stakeholder groups

For some years now, the inadequacy of the education and training system has been put forward by successive governments as one of the the main explanations of Britain's economic decline (Merson, 1995). This perceived inadequacy has been put forward as one of the major reasons behind the UK Government's attempts to shift the balance of power between the major stakeholders in vocational education and training.

The identification of vocational education and training as the explanation for Britain's economic decline led to the replacement of many of the liberal aims of education by the view that education 'must first serve the needs of the economy' (Merson, 1995), and it also enabled the Government to 'incorporate employers as new and "responsible" partners in the education and training spheres in spite of the historical evidence of employers' neglect of training'. (Merson, 1995). Certainly a central thrust of the 1997 Dearing report on the future of higher education in the UK was described by Dearing himself as being 'responsibility towards the economy' (Meikle and Major, 1997).

Open learning and new providers

The change in the relative importance of the core stakeholders came about as a result of deliberate government policy. A series of Government White Papers during the 1980s focused on the reform of training and vocational education.

> The new markets and technologies require a more highly skilled, better educated and more mobile workforce in which a much larger number of professional and technical staff are supported by a range of more or less highly trained workers who perform a range of tasks and who are involved in a process rather than the repetitive assembly or manufacture of a specific product (MSC, 1981, cited in Merson, 1995).

Example 2.3: The Open Tech Programme 1981–87

The aim of this programme was to meet skills shortages by encouraging the development of training opportunities for adults through open learning. Open learning ideas and materials were developed and disseminated through local projects which were funded on a 'pump-priming basis'. A central unit selected the local projects, monitored then and had oversight of their management. High priority was given to the needs of high technology companies and small businesses. Nearly 140 projects were developed and funded as part of the programme.

The main objectives of the programme were:

1. to make training available to meet current skill shortages, both qualitative and quantitative

2. to help companies and individuals adapt to technological change, thereby facilitating the introduction of new technologies

3. to help individuals improve their levels of skill and career prospects through training designed to meet individual circumstances, with appropriate tutorial support, guidance and counselling.

The various bodies involved in these projects included validating bodies, employers associations, industrial training boards(ITBs), non-statutory training organizations (NSTOs) and trade unions. 'As well as leading to the development and delivery of OL provisions, these projects were intended by the OTU (Open Tech Unit) to raise the profile of OL in such bodies and assist its diffusion within industrial training arrangements'.

Source: The Tavistock Institute of Human Relations (1987)

The introduction of the Open Tech programme in 1981 highlighted the shift in the focus of government training attention away from its previous emphasis on the unemployed towards employers' needs and the training needs of those already in employment (Example 2.3).

A review at the time recommended that training should be more closely related to current demand from employers and highlighted the need to open up training to the employed as well as the unemployed (The Tavistock Institute of Human Relations, 1987). The programme was to pump-prime projects which used open learning delivery methods in order to meet the needs of certain target groups.

A new framework for qualifications

At the same time, the recognition of the need for a coherent framework of qualifications, which were more easily understood by employers and employees alike, led to the government's review of vocational qualifications in 1986. This led to the establishment of a national body, the National Council for Vocational Qualifications which was intended to reform and rationalize existing qualifications 'into a single comprehensive framework' (Calder and Newton, 1995). The setting of National Targets for Education and Training in 1991 by the CBI, also involved responses from the government and the Trade Union Congress.

Moving from public to private provision

Following up on the work of the Open Tech, the Open College was set up by the British Government in 1987. 'Pump-priming' funding was provided for a period of three years, with the instruction from government that it should become self-financing after that time. The intention was that the college should, in effect, act as an agency, with a small central team offering for sale open learning materials developed by existing producers, which would then be bought and delivered by open learning centres located in further education colleges and within companies (Temple, 1991). Unfortunately, the unrealistic financial constraints, combined with a shortage of suitable products and the dependence of the College on third party delivery, proved unsustainable in its planned form. However, its pioneering work on ways of structuring materials in order to offer learners credits towards vocational qualifications were very much in tune with current thinking about occupational competencies and work-based assessment (Temple, 1991).

TECs (Training and Enterprise Councils) were introduced at the local level in 1992 to set locally agreed targets as part of the National Targets for the Education and Training initiative. The TECs, while primarily composed of local business representatives (two-thirds), were also intended to include representatives from the public sector, education, local trade unions and voluntary organizations. They played a key funding role locally, acting as government agents for the allocation of contracts and associated funds to training providers – both private and public – on the basis of competitive tendering for the delivery of a number of different government training programmes. However, there were continuing concerns about the training standards of courses funded through TECs and about the potential for fraud. In 1997, the Training Standards Council was set up by the new government to lead a crack-down on poor quality training courses in the workplace with a team of 400 part-time inspectors to scrutinize the work of the 79 TECs.

> The creation of the new council followed repeated criticisms of standards and allegations of financial mismanagement... [and]... ineffiecient use of public funds. The TECs were recently criticized by the Government when the Public Accounts Committee accused them of 'incorrect payments' of £8.6 m to training providers in 1995–6. However most of the criticisms have been aimed not at the TECs but at the private training providers recruited with public money by the councils. The quality of many national vocational qualifications awarded through TEC-sponsored work-based training was often criticised. Standards were attacked for not being on a par with other education and training options (Nash, 1997).

The Further and Higher Education Act of 1992 introduced fundamental changes to the FE system. Colleges were taken out of Local Education Authority control and became independent incorporated institutions, responsible to the Secretary of State and governed by autonomous governing bodies drawn from the local 'great and good'. Funding regimes changed, with greater emphasis on demand-led funding, and subsequently on student retention and successful completion of courses and acquisition of qualifications.

The official encouragement of a wider range of private sector training providers to provide competition for the public sector continued.

> The White Paper 'Employment for the 1990s' (HMSO 1989) placed emphasis on meeting local training needs. At incorporation TECS were given representation on college governing bodies ('Education and Training for the 21st Century' (HMSO 1990) as well as providing funding for NVQs, which, being based on assessment of the outcomes of learning, require flexibility in mode, duration and location of learning and contribute to the development of individualized learning programmes (Willmot and McLean, 1994).

The move to workplace assessment has accelerated the trend for the delivery of vocational qualifications to move away from the colleges and towards companies. A large number of companies have now been approved as assessment centres with many of the retail chain stores, hotels and catering organizations delivering the lower NVQ levels (Raggatt, 1993).

It could be argued that the changes which occurred in terms of new stakeholders in vocational education and training, and the changes in the relative importance of existing stakeholders, owed more to government ideological distaste for trade unions and for public provision and rather less to their stated preference for lack of government intervention (Trade Union membership fell by four million members during the period 1979–90). Certainly, the introduction of the Open Tech Programme, the Open College, and the TECs, the emphasis on employers' responsibility for training, the squeezing out of local authorities and of trade unions from involvement in the FE sector, and the encouragement of the private sector provision of vocational education and training through open, flexible and distance means, while aimed at opening up access to and the adoption of new forms of training, nevertheless also 'saw off' a number of the then Conservative Government's traditional opponents.

There now appears to be a strong argument for the need for coherence and stability to be recognized by government. 'It is hard to bring to mind any other national VET system that has undergone changes of such sustained pace and profundity' (Keep, 1990). At present, however, there is little sign of that happening. Shortly after becoming Britain's new Prime Minister, Tony Blair was rumoured to have asked the British chairman of the Ford Motor Company to act as a senior adviser to the Government's scheme for setting up a University for Industry to improve education in the workplace. It was reported at the time that:

> Ministers have been particularly impressed with Ford's Employee Development Assistance Programme (Edap) offering all staff the opportunity of adult education. Onsite courses are free and workers can claim up to £200 a year to offset the costs of external courses which need not be linked to their work... (Carvel, 1997).

The appointment of the chairman of the electronics giant Motorola as the head of the government advisory group to draft 'a blueprint' of the University for Industry (Nash, 1997a) further signalled the government's intention of continuing to involve employers closely in the development of a national training policy.

Changes within stakeholder groups

Government

The government departments in the UK involved in the promotion and use of open, flexible and distance approaches to vocational education and training have had a chequered history. Prior to 1979, the Department of Education and Science (DES) had the main responsibility for vocational education and training. The first major change was the announcement that a new body, the Manpower Services Commission (MSC), was now expected to play a key role (Example 2.4). The MSC was a quango, part of the Department of Employment group, most of whose staff were part of the Civil Service (*The Tavistock*, 1987).

Example 2.4: Location of responsibilities for vocational education within the civil service

The Department of Employment took a substantial stake in education and training through the Manpower Services Commission. Initially focusing on training for adults who had left school and college in1982 it was charged with introducing and managing curriculum reform in schools through the Technical and Vocational Education Initiative (TVEI) and later assumed responsibility for 25 per cent of further education funding. The Department of Trade and Industry's speciality was 'enterprise', contributing to curriculum innovation in schools through Understanding British Industry (UBI) and to the re-education of teachers through Teachers into Business and Industry. The Department of Education and Science, chastened by these incursions into its domain, proclaimed the economic purposes of education and launched its own initiatives, PICKUP, the National Curriculum, and GCSE, to name but a few.

Source: Raggatt (1993)

As Raggatt points out, after the MSC became involved, the Department of Trade and Industry also entered the scene. Thus over the last 20 years, training has been the responsibility of the then Department of Education and Science, then of various departments within the Department of Employment, and subsequently of the Department for Education and Employment (DfEE) (Example 2.5).

The fate of the Manpower Services Commission is a good example of the speed of changes during this period. During its lifetime (it was abolished by the Government in 1988, nine years after its formation) it hosted a number of initiatives and innovative programmes in vocational education and training. Renamed the 'Training Commission' in 1988, it then became the Training Agency (1989), and then the Training, Employment and Enterprise Directorate of the Employment Department. However, the commitment by government to open and flexible learning as an important solution to vocational education and training problems has continued throughout. Even after the change of government in 1997, the new Labour Government included a financial commitment to a 'University for Industry' in its first budget.

The primary interest of any government in any policy change or development must be a political one. Sometimes *ad hoc* solutions to events must be found. Certainly some authorities argue that 'the political necessity for the government to be seen to act swiftly and decisively to tackle problems' during the youth unemployment crisis of the early 1980s was one of the major reasons for the lack of any attempt to design a vocational education and training system from first principles (Kushner, 1985, cited in (Keep, 1990)). The UK Government during the 1980s and early 1990s had a clear interest in employer-led vocational education – a position which fitted in with their commitment to deregulation and increasing labour market flexibility.

Example 2.5: Key training initiatives introduced by government:

1979   Responsibility for training moved from the Department of Education and Science (DES) to the MSC (Manpower Services Commission)

1980   MSC review of the 1973 Employment and Training Act shifts responsibility for funding training towards industry

1981   Abolition of 24 Industrial Training Boards; Consultative document, *A New Training Initiative*, published by the MSC: stressed need for flexible workforce, permanent national comprehensive training programme for all young people, concept of occupational competence

1982   The MSC report, *The Youth Task Group Report*, proposes the Youth Training Scheme (YTS – introduced in 1983)

1983   MSC Report *Towards an Adult Training Strategy*

1984   Introduction of the Non-Advanced Further Education Initiative (NAFE)

1986   National Council for Vocational Qualifications set up following publication of White Paper *Review of Vocational Qualifications in England and Wales* (MSC/DES)

1987   Open College launched by the MSC to become an independent educational trust

1988   Government abolishes the MSC. Sets up the Training Agency; the Job Training Scheme for adults replaced by 'Employment Training'; White Paper, *Employment for the 1990s*, from the Employment Department

1991   White Paper, *Education and Training for the 21st Century*, from the Department of Education and Science and Employment Department Group

1992   NVQs introduced; 82 TECs (22 LECs in Scotland), set up by the Department for Trade and Industry; FE Colleges taken out of LEA control

1994   'Modern Apprenticeships' introduced following the White Paper on *Competitiveness*

1997   Employment Department and Department for Education combined into Department for Education and Employment; University for Industry Pilot Schemes set up

Employers

While the government has assumed a causal relationship between the level of vocational education and training and the economic health of the country, the same logic has clearly not been applied by many employers in relation to their companies.

The downsizing and reorganization of training departments, together with the reorganization of responsibilities for in-company training, appear to suggest that this area of activity is, in many companies, still seen as a cost rather than as an investment.

> When firms were asked why they did not carry out more training, they cited time and cost as the principal reasons. British and German companies were the most likely in Europe to see cost as a factor more training [*sic*]. More than half the British companies felt that lack of time was a barrier (Crequer, 1997b).

> ... most of the organizations [approached] were undergoing major reorganizations of their training and development programmes. With training programmes in a state of transition and uncertainty, and with reorganization signifying retrenchment in many cases, the project [on the effectiveness of open and flexible learning in vocational education] was seen to touch upon a politically sensitive area (Calder *et al.*, 1995).

At the same time, the reorganizations seen in UK Government departments over the past 20 years or so is simply a reflection of what has been happening in companies for rather longer. It is now almost 30 years since Toffler (1970), in reference to the 'tide of mergers and de-mergers' described how 'organizations now change their internal shape with a frequency – and sometimes a rashness – that makes the head swim'. John Gardner defined the 'self-renewing' organization as one which constantly changed its structure in response to changing needs (Gardner, 1963). Major internal reorganizations continue to be a frequent occurrence within large corporations, although they are frequently reluctant to publicize them. At the same time, the old hierarchical management structures have changed. Responsibilities change rapidly, new ways of working come and go. For example, workers may well have a number of different bosses in a 'matrix' organization – an administrative boss plus separate project bosses. Complexity within companies brings with it new forms of responsibilities for staff.

Companies who do invest in training may follow the route of providing their own training, or be consumers of training provided by external agencies, or use a mix of the two. For example, in the UK, the Post Office buys in training from external providers as well as directly from its own training people (see Case Study 2.3).

Buying in training from external providers, or 'outsourcing', has been increasing, with large companies twice as likely to contract out services as other businesses at around 36 per cent who do so. Over one-third of larger firms contract out services to outside suppliers (Institute of Personnel and Development survey on employment issues, October 1996, cited in Denny, 1997). An increasing number of those services which are now contracted out used to be performed in-house, including the training function. It should perhaps be mentioned that there are now increasing doubts about the overall benefits which contracting out brings to the client organization. Management theorists 'have begun to recognise that, even in the private

---

Case Study 2.3: Post Office

Training provision within the company
Each of the four major companies which now form the Post Office have their own
training section. In addition, the Training and Development Group provide training
on an internal recharge basis directly to Post Office clients, sometimes in competition
with other providers, as well as providing a support and consultancy service to their
own training sections. Open and flexible learning provision is part of the support
service to other training sections. At present, the role of the Group is undergoing
some change as it moves to working more in partnership with Post Office businesses
and helping them to achieve their business objectives. The transitional phase is
expected to last for a couple of years.

---

sector, the process has in some areas become self-defeating – and that firms need
to retain significant internal capacity themselves. Contract out too much, they warn,
and you no longer know what you are doing, let alone what your contractor is up
to' (Milne and Michie, 1997).

Training that is bought from external providers may be designed specifically for
the company, or may be training which is available to anyone. To a certain extent
this will depend on where the decision-making about training policy lies within a
company. The reality is that 'employers' are not just some homogeneous entity, or
set of organizations. Even organizations of similar sizes, which cover similar
geographical areas, and which deal in the same industrial or commercial sector, may
have a very different decision-making structure where training is concerned, and
as a result, will have different types of staff involved in making key training decisions
on their behalf. Thus, within companies, the education and training stakeholders
may be:

- board members
- departmental heads
- line managers/supervisors
- personnel/human resource managers
- company training managers
- site training managers.

The very diversity of the location of responsibility for the training function in
different companies and for spending on training, makes it very difficult to get
reliable data on the full range and extent of training currently taking place in industry
and commerce. Of companies who do provide training for their employees (NOP
[1992]):

- 23 per cent have a specialist training department
- 24 per cent employ training instructors
- 20 per cent use an internal training officer

- 30 per cent used external training consultants
- 52 per cent other

While training policy may need board level approval, the actual strategies which are used to implement policy may be decided at a much lower level. The refocusing of training responsibilities appears to owe much to the increasing use of regular staff appraisals and to the Investors in People Initiative (IiP). IiP was intended to be a tool that would improve business performance and emphasize the importance to businesses of their staff. To gain IiP status, 'employers must show commitment to staff development, and that employee training is linked to business goals. They must provide induction training for all new staff, and review training needs' (Merrick, 1997). It has been claimed by the scheme's organizers that more than one in four employees are now involved in the IiP scheme. 'IiP has set itself the aim of persuading more than 70 per cent of large employers and 35 per cent of medium-sized organisations to adopt the standard by the year 2000 (Wylie, 1997). However, by 1996 only 8 per cent of organizations employing 200 or more employees and 5 per cent of those employing 50 or more were Investors in People (DfEE, 1996).

Line managers now play a key role in identifying staff training and development needs during staff appraisal sessions. The quality of the links between the line managers and the training organizers are thus key to the provision of training which meets the needs of the member of staff. Just as the quality of the links between the training organizer and those responsible for the training policy within the organization will determine the relevance and effectiveness of the policy for the company's needs.

Training providers

Considerable competition between public and private providers of open, flexible and distance approaches to training has emerged over the past few years. The major public providers in the UK have been the FE colleges, although there are a number of other types of public sector providers such as universities and local education authorities (see Table 2.1).

It is among the providers of training that there has probably been some of the greatest changes over the past three decades. The recognition of the potential of open and distance learning to open up access to higher education has been achieved by the success of the Open University. Discussions about an 'OU analogue' in the FE field took place at the then Department for Education and Science in the mid-1970s. The projects, developed under the MSC-initiated and funded Open Tech programme, drew in a significantly wide range of organizations. What in effect was happening was the beginning of the widening of training provision towards a much greater contribution from the private sector. Employers were now expected to contribute to the costs of training. The expectation was that the sales to employers of training packages and services developed through the Open Tech programme would enable Open Learning to become self-financing (Example 2.6).

Table 2.1 *Organizations involved in sponsoring materials development projects for the Open Tech Programme*

Types of sponsoring organization	Materials development projects	
	N	%
Total*	86	100
Universities	19	22
FE Colleges	29	33
LEAs	7	8
Other educational organization	7	8
Company or firm	10	12
Employers association	11	13
Professional association	4	5
ITB	8	9
Training association	10	12
Validating body	5	6
Trade union	3	3

Note: some projects were sponsored by more than one organization

Source: *The Tavistock* (1987)

Example 2.6: Open Tech programme

The aims of the Open Tech Programme are to cater for:

- industrial sectors: manufacturing industry, banking and finance, retail and distribution, transport and communications.

- occupational groups: technicians and supervisors, managers and craft workers

- high technology training needs: electronics and computing in general, CAD/CAM, office automation, energy managment and control, quality assurance and control

- small businesses

- 'special groups' such as women, members of ethnic minorities, and the unemployed.

Source: *The Tavistock* (1987)

Changes in the balance between public and private provision have continued. 'The broad market figures are that there are around 4000 private training providers registered with TECS compared with around 350 colleges' (Hoare, 1997). However, these 350 colleges provided education and training to 3.5 million students in 1995/96 – an overall increase of 16 per cent over the previous year. The vast majority of these students were part time and were funded by public funds (75 per cent and 77 per cent respectively). The number of private training providers in the UK, who offer distance education options, however, is rather difficult to establish. The 294 distance education providers listed in the ICDL UK directory of Distance Learning and Supported Open Learning comprise both public and private providers, but do not include within-company provision (ICDL, 1997a).

FE Colleges have undergone a challenging series of changes since they were removed from Local Education Authority control in 1992. Their funding regimes have been modified several times, increasingly focusing on completion and successful achievement of qualifications. In spite of the huge growth in the student numbers being dealt with by the FE sector, the pressures are still very much on FE Colleges to reduce costs while increasing student numbers. Staff salaries and working hours are now locally determined. For many staff, new conditions have actually brought increased hours and, for some, cuts in salary resulting in reports such as 'Strikes could hit a West Country college as lecturers refuse to sign new contracts that would increase hours and cut pay' appearing in national newspapers (Thomson, 1997).

Meanwhile, both full- and part-time student numbers within FE Colleges continue to rise rapidly.

> With the FEFC [Further Education Funding Council] offer of 15 per cent funding increase for colleges achieving 15 per cent growth in student numbers between 1993 and 1995, colleges are being asked to improve efficiency at the same time as increasing flexibility (Willmot and McLean, 1994).

Further changes to supervisory and regulatory bodies in 1997 further exacerbated the competition between private training providers and colleges. To a certain extent, the boundaries between public and private providers are becoming increasingly blurred. Many colleges are operating increasingly in the commercial world, pushed both by the need to identify appropriate work-based training for their students, and by the need to supplement their increasingly tight budgets.

The students and trainees

The distinction between vocational and non-vocational adult education has long been made within the British system of post-school education in spite of the problems this involves. Courses in office management or computer programming can be and often are undertaken by people wishing to organize their affairs at home more efficiently, or to 'keep their brains active' as well as by those intending to use their new skills in their jobs. The reason it is important to recognize that this distinction is still made by stakeholders is that it can substantially affect the way in which figures on participation are interpreted. It can also affect the extent to which those involved directly in training for business and industry, and those involved in publicly sponsored adult education, communicate and learn from each other.

For example, as we saw earlier, three-quarters of all adults who had completed their full-time education had participated in some form of learning over the previous three years (Beinhart and Smith, 1998). The numbers involved in job-related training are somewhat lower, at around 67 per cent, with almost six in ten (58 per cent) undertaking taught courses. The proportion involved in open, flexible and distance learning is clearly lower, but a surprisingly high proportion – 29 per cent of taught learning – involved working alone from packages of materials. It is likely, however, that a considerably smaller proportion than this actually came from manual level occupations than from non-manual jobs.

Who participates?

Post-school participation in any form of education or training varies considerably between different groups within society. Providers of adult education in Western Europe and the US have, for many years, been more than aware of the limited appeal of their courses for any but the 'relatively affluent, well-educated, white, middle-class individual' (Brookfield, 1986). In terms of the question 'who gets involved in education and training?', there is considerable consensus between the different studies in the US and in Western Europe. The evidence on job-related training among employed people in the UK reflects very much the pattern previously identified for adult learning in general, that is, those who are already well educated or trained are most likely to be the ones who continue to receive it. In other words, the most significant predictor of whether an adult will participate in formal education and training is previous educational attainment and participation.

The participants in our own study were not intended to be representative of trainees and students in general who were undertaking vocational education. Our aim was to include a variety of different types of courses. In so doing, however, we succeeded in including a wide range of students and trainees in terms of age and occupational status and type. However, the majority did share one characteristic. Although 74 per cent of the participants in our study had left school at age 16 or earlier, 94 per cent had some form of qualification – only 6 per cent of them had no qualifications at all. The rest had a variety of NVQs (4 per cent), GCSEs (62 per cent), BTecs and other qualifications. About half of the participants had undertaken some other course or form of training in the last three years; the majority of it by part-time study. Previous training had included a variety of different media and teaching components. Those participants who were currently doing courses or training, which were termed traditional, were more likely to have had recent experience involving group work on another course (78 per cent) than were those currently being trained through OFL (68 per cent).

As regards employment status, the students and trainees included both employed and unemployed people, with only half of our participants in full-time paid employment. Unemployed participants were found equally on traditional courses and those on courses being studied by open, flexible or distance means. There was a good spread of ages among our participants. While the majority were under 40, 20 per cent of the sample were in their 40s or older. The youngest students were most likely to be using open, flexible or distance methods (see Table 2.2). The gender representation was roughly equal, with equal proportions of male and female studying both traditional courses and open, flexible and distance courses.

Table 2.2 *Age distribution of study participants (OFL n= 238; Traditional n= 264)*

	OFL %	Traditional %
16–19	35	26
20–29	22	27
30–39	23	22
40–49	16	20
50–	4	3

The missing groups

The groups who are missing from the education and training picture are described by Hillman (1996) in his review of relevant research:

> Other evidence shows that other groups systematically participated less in formal learning, notably the unemployed, the self employed, flexible workers (disproportionately female) who lack the alliegence of an employer, older workers, ethnic minorities, those with domestic responsibilities, the disabled, and those in certain industrial sectors and regions.

The study by Beinhart *et al.* carried out in 1997 tells the same story. Those least likely to participate in vocational training are unskilled manual workers (half the participation rate of professional/managerial workers), older workers and women. Significantly, those adults (primarily women) who stay at home to look after a family are only half as likely as even registered unemployed to have taken part in some vocational training during the previous three years (Beinhart and Smith, 1998).

These then are the people who feature in other analyses of those who miss out within today's society – the groups which Hutton has called the disadvantaged, the marginalized and the insecure – the 30 per cent of the adult working population who are either unemployed, economically inactive, or on government schemes who comprise the disadvantaged, together with the further 30 per cent in part-time casual and temporary work who comprise the marginalized and the insecure (Hutton, 1996). The problem is that for many people, their insecurity has become a way of life.

Nearly two-fifths of the unemployed have been without work for more than a year. They bear most of the hardship of joblessness: the discouragement, loss of self-esteem and atrophy of skills. One fifth of working-age households has nobody working (Snower, 1997).

At the same time, some groups are disproportionately affected by unemployment (see the annual Labour Force Survey). For example, the unemployment rate for members of ethnic minorities is double the rate for whites and rates for young adults are higher than for those over 25, although over the last few years, the changing population age profile has meant that increasing numbers of young people have been coming on to the job market.

Young people have been targeted in numerous government schemes. However, many stakeholders are critical about the seeming lack of results. For example in their report *Working to Learn*, the Institute of Personnel and Development concludes that 'simply tinkering with the present mechanisms would lead to "initiative fatigue"'. In spite of the many different youth training programmes during the 1980s, they claim that the results are:

- young people who want nothing more to do with formalized learning
- a society which has low expectations of what many young people can achieve
- an implicit belief that many are destined for unemployment or for a life of low-skill work that needs little or no preparation
- cynicism – 'often well founded' – about the quality of government training schemes aimed at the unemployed
- jobs that offer no training
- patchy demands from employers for a general upskilling of the workforce.

The researchers blamed the commitment to market-based education for creating low expectations, and argued that competition between schools, and schools and colleges, and colleges and employers had been wasteful, and that '... over-emphasis on individual responsibility for learning 'dangerously ignores wider issues of social justice'. The report suggested that employers should be prosecuted if they do not train the young people they take on (Crequer, 1997).

Self-directed learners

The concern about the lack of participation in training by certain groups reflects the very similar concerns expressed at one time by adult educators. It was not until the late 1970s that research, first in the US and then in Canada, reveal that, in fact, a wide range of adults did engage in a great deal of learning, but that this learning took place outside formal settings, and was planned and organized by the learners themselves. The first study to identify the existence of what later became known as the 'iceberg' of adult learning activities was carried out by Johnstone and Rivera in 1965. They carried out a national questionnaire survey in the US which provided empirical evidence of the fact that adults can and do organize their own learning activities and that these frequently took place outside formal classrooms and courses.

The phenomenon of self-directed learning became the subject of a significant number of studies over the next 20 years. The latest national UK study provided further evidence of the importance of this form of learning. Over half (57 per cent) of respondents had undertaken some non-taught learning in the previous three years (Beinhart and Smith, 1998). Around 30 per cent had had supervised training while actually doing a job, 51 per cent had been keeping up to date with developments related to their work, and 29 per cent had been trying to improve their knowledge without undertaking a taught course. Only 1 per cent had studied in this way for some form of qualification (Beinhart and Smith, 1998).

The term 'self-directed learning' is used in two rather different ways in the literature. The first one refers to the process of learning, and describes the fact that the learning is planned, organized, carried out and evaluated by the learner. 'The learner chooses what to learn and how to learn, as well as when and where to learn, what resources to use, and how much to learn. The learner also decides when to continue and when to end the learning project and determines whether the results were adequate' (Mocker and Spear, 1982, cited in Berger, 1990). Used in this way, self-directed learning is simply an alternative to what might be termed 'other-directed' forms of learning such as are traditionally used in formal education and training. The other use of the term refers to the self-directed learner as a person with certain personal attributes. The assumption here is that some people possess these attributes, to a greater or lesser extent, while others do not. Those who possess these attributes are seen as more likely to be able to undertake self-directed learning successfully than will those who do not posses them, or who possess them to only a limited degree.

The amount of self-directed learning which people undertake has been put at around 10–14 hours on average each week (Tough, 1979). The rash of follow-up studies which followed all supported the conclusion that the majority of people's learning efforts are undertaken without professional help. 'Education and training which is undertaken in formal structured settings is not an attractive proposition for disaffected adults. In contrast, they are comfortable with the learning that they undertake themselves and which they organize independently, even though it is largely unrecognised and rarely valued by others' (Calder, 1993). The development of new forms of assessment which recognize prior learning and which enable training to take account of skills acquired in non-formal settings therefore allows those with little previous success within the education system to have their achievements formally recognized. At the same time, it is clear that in principle, open learning, with its emphasis on access and its recognition of learners' needs to have greater control over their learning, should hold a greater appeal among those groups who have been less represented on the more conventional courses. Research evidence on this is mixed. Woodley (1993) concludes that the great majority of OU students with low qualifications have already taken other courses since leaving school. As he points out, good distance teaching materials in themselves are unlikely to retain learners who are already disaffected with education. Good admissions' counselling to alert students to what they are taking on, together with appropriate help and support throughout their studies are likely to be an essential part of the overall provision (Case Study 2.4).

Case Study 2.4: The Strathclyde experiment

The Strathclyde experiment targeted disadvantaged learners. The participants, using highly structured independent learning materials, are supported intensively within local community groups. As Marian Lever reports 'The key ingredients seem to be small and achievable tasks frequently presented to reinforce success and some prestigious recognition of that success... we try throughout the process to shift the emphasis from the tutor to the student to reinforce their potential as a learning resource for themselves and others.

Source: Lever (1993)

The learners and trainees included in our own study did include a good mix of employed and unemployed. However, the relatively high level of people with at least some form of qualification was probably a result, at least in part, of the relatively youthful nature of our sample. Although there were older people, there was a distinct bias towards younger people. However, the gender split and the relative lack of previous training experience for half the sample do suggest that the sample included many of those groups which have been targeted by various government schemes.

As mentioned previously, the balance of power between different stakeholders in vocational education and training has been shifting substantially. These changes, however, have taken place at a time when major changes within stakeholder groups have also been occurring. The lack of a clearly agreed policy to provide a common aim and clear strategy has meant that even among the specially targeted groups the, admittedly limited, evidence suggests that there has been differential success in reaching them. Certainly, their greatly varying needs have presented other stakeholder groups with a formidable challenge. It may be, however, that the mode of study can make a difference in facilitating more effectively targeted provision. The next chapter will examine the reasons why different stakeholders adopt open and distance methods for vocational education and training; the objectives which vocational education and training programmes using open, flexible and distance methods are expected to meet and the constraints within which training solutions have to be found. In particular, Chapter 3 will also look at the learning skills which students have to bring with them.

Chapter 3

What problem is being solved?

This chapter investigates the rationale behind the decisions to go for open and distance education options in terms of the objectives towards which policy-makers, training managers and trainers have to work. Much is made of the need for companies to be able to adapt if they are to continue to compete. In particular the need for international competitiveness is constantly reiterated by government. Employers need to recruit workers with the skills they need to run their businesses effectively, and need to be able to train them effectively and efficiently. The notion of competency has also had a profound effect on the thinking behind the design and provision of training courses ((Mabey and Iles, 1994). The effect has been to refocus the judgement of training courses from knowledge and skills acquisition, to knowledge and skills application.

This chapter also examines the problems to which training using open, flexible and distance methods can be seen as a solution by focusing on the needs of the different stakeholders. The extent to which those needs may conflict or may coincide and in what sort of circumstances will be discussed.

Human capital

In the early 1960s, labour market economists recognized that there is a relationship between what people spend on themselves and the benefits which they enjoy as a result in both the short and the long term. They developed from this the concept of human capital. This relationship is perhaps most generally recognized in the field of health where, increasingly, people 'spend' time, self-control, energy and cash today in order to experience benefits to their health in the future. They have taken heed of the old jazzplayer's comment 'If I'd known I was going to live this long, I'd have taken better care of myself'.

In the field of education and training, the concept of human capital has been used to argue that the direct and indirect costs of education and its anticipated financial benefits affect the size of the demand for education (Blaug, 1992, cited in Tight, 1996). In fact, the financial benefits of a first degree, for example, are seen to be so clear that they were used by the British Government to justify the introduction of tuition fees to students in the higher education sector as from 1998.

Tight (1996) highlights the work of both Schultz and Johnes in relation to the distinction between general and specific human capital.

> Distinctions may be drawn between general and specific human capital, with the former applying to 'skills and knowledge which enhances the worker's productivity, regardless of where she is employed', and the latter to 'skills which can be productively used only by the worker's current employer (Johnes, 1993:14–15). The clear implication is that the latter will be of most concern to the employer, who will tend to see it as wasteful to educate employees for potential employment elsewhere. General human capital development is seen as being chiefly the concern of the state or community, through its provision of general education and training.

No distinction is made here about the status of the workers involved. There is an emphasis in the literature on human capital on management training, so it is unclear to what extent the distinction between specific and general development is seen as applying to the lower levels or the basic staff grades. Certainly within those companies with a national reputation in the training field such as Ford, Rover, and IBM, provision is made for general development of all grades of staff as well as specific development.

General versus specific training does vary even between competitors in the same field. For example, studies carried out in the period 1993–95 revealed that two major national food retailers, Safeway and Tesco, both used similar competency-based induction training through open learning methods for their store staff. But whereas Safeway trained staff to become Safeway employees, assessing only the specific set of competencies judged necessary for working within a Safeways store, anticipating that they would stay with the company for some considerable time, Tesco's offered assessment for the award of NVQs to their shop floor staff, giving them the opportunity to acquire 'portable' qualifications (Case Study 3.1).

Although an increasing number of employers are offering staff the opportunity to acquire qualifications, this is still relatively rare, particularly for lower grades of staff. In fact, as Table 3.1 shows, a lower proportion of the employer-funded spells of learning are directed towards a qualification than are self-funded spells of learning. This suggests that Johnes' interpretation that the interest of employers may tend to be in specific human capital rather than in general human capital may have some validity (Johnes, 1993, cited in Tight, 1995).

Case Study 3.1: Examples of general and specific development

Safeway: Competency-based training programmes have been implemented for all retail staff at Safeway. Store assistants training is referred to as the Head Start Programme. It is store based and involves a combination of on the job instruction, training videos and specially written handbooks. The head start programme is designed for all new employees joining Safeway stores and it sets out the training which must be undertaken within the first 12 weeks of employment. It covers induction, core and basic skills and the training programme provides a checklist of all the skills and knowledge a new employee needs to learn and use during the first 12 weeks of employment.

Core training therefore takes place through work activities overseen by the department manager who acts as 'mentor' and also carries out supervision and competency assessment. On satisfactory completion of all the required competencies, staff receive an increase in their wages.[1]

Tesco: As of March 1995, 350 staff had achieved an NVQ, mostly for Retail level 1 or 2, with over 1,500 employees (1.4 per cent of the total workforce) currently working towards an NVQ. The aim of the company is to achieve their target of 10 per cent of employees working towards this qualification. All staff, whether full-time or part-time, in all stores, are to have access to an NVQ in Retail levels 1 and 2... While participation on the company training programmes was an essential aspect of employee's work, registration for NVQs was entirely voluntary. However considerable effort at the store level went into exhorting staff to register for the Retail NVQ.[2]

Sources:
[1]Calder *et al.* (1995)
[2]Calder and Newton (1995)

Table 3.1 *Funding sources of learning*

Percentage of spells of learning directed towards a qualification or module, by funding source %.

Self-funded	56
Employer-funded	38
Employer-arranged (no funding necessary)	15

Source: ED/SCPR (1994) cited in Department for Education and Employment (1996)

Employers' problems

Changes in attitudes to stakeholders

Some industry leaders appear to join with government in arguing that sustained business success results from a rather different stakeholder model than that operated currently by many companies. They argue that:

> ... companies should reduce their focus on shareholders and give more weight to other stakeholders such as employees, customers and suppliers... (Cowe and Buckingham, 1994).

In the same report John Neill, Chief Executive of Unipart, commented:

> Many in business have grown up with the idea that short-term, power-based relationships with stakeholders are the route to competitive advantage. But there is a better model, which is in harmony with capitalism, which has long-term relationships with stakeholders and with society...
>
> In developed economies, skilled service workers will form the majority of the labour force. Tomorrow's company has to learn how to derive the greatest competitive advantage from these groups.

The benefits of this approach were unexpectedly illustrated by Sir Anthony Cleaver, chairman of IBM in the UK and chair of the team who produced the report, when he admitted that:

> more than 40 per cent of IBM UK's workforce had lost their jobs in the past three years. But he said that the company's emphasis on training and employee development – its 'inclusive approach' – meant all these cuts were voluntary. 'The people were highly employable elsewhere' he said (Cowe and Buckingham, 1994).

In this instance, worker flexibility and transferability to other employers was clearly seen as a benefit by a major employer when set against the sort of problems that normally accompany the scale of 'downsizing', which was undertaken here.

Conforming to regulations

Conformity to regulatory practices appears to be another trigger for the provision of general human capital development in that workers may have to acquire a recognized qualification, which has a transferable value. Health and safety certificates are one example. Another example comes from the world of finance where compliance with such UK regulatory authorities as the Personal Investment Authority (PIA) means that sellers of regulated financial products need to demonstrate certain competences and acquire specified certification (Case Study 3.2).

Case Study 3.2: TSB

TSB is a retail bank that employs some 16,000 staff and has a national network of 1200 branches. The Personal Investment Authority (PIA) is the regulatory body that controls and minitors the standards relating to the sale of regulated products such as life assurance, pensions and investment products. To meet the PIA's standards of competency, sellers of regulated products need to demonstrate sales competency through the completion of Financial Planning Certificates 1, 2, and 3. Open learning was selected as the lead methodology through which staff would study to attain the required competences primarily because it would reduce the need to take people out of the business for training (reducing the associated opportunity costs), and could maximize the value provided from the Retail Training budget.

Source: adapted from (Higgins, 1997)

Even where there is no external regulatory body, a major employer may see benefits from being able to assure customers that service staff have all been accredited as possessing a minimum level of competence. However, the need for even basic grade staff to have recognized qualifications, which attest their competences in a set of skills, has led to employers experiencing considerable difficulties in recruiting appropriately qualified people (Case Study 3.3).

Case Study 3.3: Severn Trent Water

Severn Trent Water is the second largest of the ten privatized UK water companies. It is a monopoly supplier of water and sewage treatment and disposal. It took a policy decision to go the NVQ route to becoming a learning organization. The decision to ask all craft and process workers to go for full NVQs was part of a strategy intended to change the culture of the organization. 'The company planned substantial downsizing. NVQs were seen as providing the technical base for a leaner, more efficient workforce...The challenge was seen by the training department as being 'one off' in that the aim was to assess nearly 3,000 craft and process workers in order to achieve a base of a skilled and qualified workforce who could achieve a guaranteed quality of output. Thereafter, new staff will be expected to achieve the appropriate levels within agreed time limits.

An open learning approach was adopted when it was found that 'although workers had many of the practical competences, they did not in many cases have the underpinning knowledge and understanding – ie, they were not able to explain why they did the work in certain ways and why different techniques were applied in different circumstances.' A special booklet was prepared which covered all the issues workers needed in order to answer the knowledge questions. This was used in conjunction with a three-day in-house course.

Source: Raggatt, cited in (Calder and Newton, 1995)

Keeping pace with change

The issue of change and of the increasing rate of change is a key issue in many sectors. It is clear that the accelerating rate of change in industry and commerce implies accelerating training needs for industry. Open learning is viewed as one of the central means by which education and training could adapt speedily to meet the needs of the economy and industry (Case Study 3.4).

Case Study 3.4: Post Office Counters Ltd

With about 600 product changes each year, the main challenge facing the training section of Post Office Counters Ltd is how to ensure the training is up-to-date and relevant. The provision of over 2,000 sets of open learning workbooks each year guarantees consistency but they are expensive to produce. The material for most of the booklets takes up to 12 months to develop. They have to be in full colour in order to allow for correct product identification by the users, although the answer booklets are in black and white, and they can easily get out of date within a few weeks. In fact a major responsibility of the trainers is to constantly ensure that the current booklet is being used. Nevertheless the workbooks are seen as providing essential support to trainers and to trainees during the initial counter training period.

Source: Calder *et al.*, (1995)

Thus, open learning is viewed as a means of providing a flexible and adaptable response to changes required by moving markets. A similar point is made by Temple (1991). Here she discusses the process of coping with change within an organization:

> … organizations whose profitability and survival depend on keeping ahead of the game have to do more than fire-fight: they must take account of the changing circumstances in their environment if they are not to become a new generation of dinosaurs. West Germany is well-known for its 'over-training' culture, that is training in anticipation of future needs to provide a reservoir of skills and abilities. However, models from other cultures do not 'take' very readily in the UK, and this is unlikely to be different. An encouraging fact is that people who have experienced open learning actually seem to be sensitized to the possibility of updating or reskilling themselves on a fairly regular basis. Here I would maintain that OL is not only assisting people to respond to change by providing them with fire-fighting equipment, it is making them more aware of the fire-fighting potential in their working environment

Certainly, there were clear examples of the type of awareness of change and of the problems associated with trying to keep abreast with change within a retail organization in our own study (Case Study 3.5).

Case Study 3.5: Trainer with a national retail organization

The business moves faster than we can come up with packages and I can't see that changing. We're so competitive, if [there is] a good idea, we put it into the stores straight away. If there's not time to produce a pack, someone will go in and support. We have computer-based training (CBT) – it was brought in with stock ordering procedures. Computer-based training keeps us up to date. We've had problems. Retail is all about people and there's resistance to learning from a computer or an active learning workbook. The workbook is open learning, the tutorial is traditional learning. When they were designed it was decided that they could not cover all the information through the workbook so they would need tutorials to support them. That's just for management trainees, its not for anyone else... CBT skills-based training is for general assistants.

Reduction of employer costs

Rumble (1997) argues that a number of different studies, including a major study by Coopers and Lybrand (1990), support the claim that open learning methods can be more cost-effective than traditional methods. They have shown that use of distance teaching methods can help reduce employers' costs by avoiding some of the costs of face-to-face teaching. Moore and Thompson (1990) and their colleagues also report on several US studies which support these conclusions.

Example 3.1: Reduction of employer costs

The Inland Revenue made a commitment to open learning about four years ago. This was driven by a need to reduce training costs. It is felt that education and training within the Inland Revenue is now more flexible. The number of staff involved in providing training have been reduced, with an estimated cost saving of approximately a third.

Source: Calder *et al.* (1995)

From Rank Xerox ... the view was expressed among those with whom we spoke that the balance would shift from live [tutor led] courses to more and more open learning and flexible courses. 'Classroom learning is expensive and it is not right for everybody'. At the same time, the investment in workshop facilities does mean that maximim utilization is needed if they are to cover their running costs.

Source: Calder *et al.* (1995)

Rumble also reports a survey in the UK of 426 employers that 'asked employers to identify which kind of employee the various approaches were most appropriate for'. While in-house training was seen as appropriate for everyone, open and distance learning was seen to be particularly suitable for middle and senior management (88 and 83 per cent respectively). The research, which was carried out for the UK Open University, confirmed that the main advantage perceived by employers for open and distance learning was that the learning could be done in the individual's own time and at their own pace (27 per cent), thus enabling individuals to work and study at the same time (20 per cent) (Rumble, 1997).

There are three important points here:

1. In the examples we have come across in our own research, staff were not expected to study in their own time. While this may be true of management level staff, it does not appear to be the case necessarily with basic levels of staff. Almost certainly this is because of historic practices whereby conventional training of basic grade staff always took place during work time. Only for longer courses such as day release, where there was a clear long-term benefit to the trainee in the way of a recognized qualification at the end of their studies, have trainees been expected to spend some of their own free time on their studies. This has meant that such staff continue to expect to train in work time, with all the problems which that entails for fitting in with work schedules and for finding appropriate space for study in the work location.
2. Perceptions of appropriateness of open learning for different levels of staff reported from the MAI study do not match the reality of the kinds of employee for whom open learning is actually provided in many companies. This may be a company specific issue in that the companies we talked to in the course of our researches were selected precisely because they were providing training for basic grade staff through open learning.
3. Cost advantage depends on a number of different decisions, in particular the right framework needs to be in place. However, Bates points out that computers and computing software are 'a difficult technology to get right' (Bates, 1995). As he points out, the improvements in both hardware and software can dramatically reduce the labour costs associated with the development and design of computer-based learning. But as technology improves, so do the range of possible applications.

Bates (1995) draws attention to three types of CBT training identified by Stahmer and Green (1993):

1. very high-end production/technology value: multi-media, in-house production
2. medium-end development: contracting with a courseware firm
3. low-end development: buying 'off-the-shelf' materials.

These figures show clearly that the effect of student numbers on unit costs is particularly marked for high-end development. Although the three types of development have been identified in relation to CBT training, the same principle of course applies to all types of open learning (see Table 3.2).

Table 3.2   *Cost per student study hour for CBT*

No. of students	Type of development		
	High-end US$	Medium-end US$	Low-end US$
0	0	0	0
150	109	34	16
250	67	22	11
500	35	14	7
625	28	11	7
1,000	19	8	5

Source: adapted from (Bates, 1995)

The costs quoted by Rumble from the Coopers and Lybrand studies add credence to Bates' conclusions. Note particularly that there is one example where distance learning is actually slightly more expensive than the equivalent training presented conventionally: this is for Delco Electronics, where the comparison is between bought-in materials supported by the in-factory open learning centre, compared with in-house training plus local college release (Rumble, 1997). However, apart from this single exception, there appears to be a strong link between the number of students for whom training is provided and the unit cost of the training, with distance methods consistently cheaper than conventional methods (see Table 3.3).

The benefits to employers of using open, flexible and distance approaches for their training appear to be clear. The developing trend of regarding employees as important stakeholders in businesses does logically carry with it the need to recognize that the 'inclusive' approach to training – the view of general training as contributing to the growth of human capital – is likely to mean offering employees the opportunity to acquire qualifications. It is claimed that staff motivation and self-esteem, particularly for the basic grade staff who may previously have only experienced failure in the formal education system, are substantially increased. At the same time, other pressures are driving employers, such as the need to cut costs, to keep pace with rapid change, and to conform to regulations.

In spite of these positive pressures, there are some key problems with which employers have to cope. For example, where an employer has invested in separate training premises, there will be pressure to maximize the use of those premises. At the same time, perceptions of what are seen as 'appropriate' approaches for different grades of staff may well unnecessarily limit possibly innovative solutions to different training problems. There may well also be resistance from staff themselves – both from those responsible for training and from those identified as needing training. Given that the need to cut costs does frequently mean that new training strategies are accompanied by downsizing, an element of suspicion among workers about employers' motives does seem historically justified.

Table 3.3 *Comparative costs per student of distance and traditional education systems*

Institution/ country	Measure of cost	Number of students	Unit cost (given currency) distance (UK£)	conventional (UK£)	Distance type
Land Rover, UK	Average cost per trainee	13	1867	2527	bought-in materials
British Gas North Western, UK	Average cost per trainee	28	1552	2691	open learning materials, tuition days and residential weekend
Scottish and Universal, UK	Average cost per trainee	40	1110	2173	bought-in materials and tutorial support
Shropshire Health Authority, UK	Average cost per trainee	15	1003	1368	pre-existing materials and day-release tutorials
The Citizen Group of Newspapers, UK	Average cost per trainee	68	627	1263	open learning packs and one-to-one
Delco Electronics, UK	Average cost per trainee	72	453*	421*	*bought-in materials and support from in-factory OL Centre 9/1/97
Mathieson's Bakers, UK	Average cost per trainee	80	295	435	shop-based open learning
Thistle Hotels, UK	Average cost per trainee	20	264	2690	bought-in materials
Triplex Safety Glass, UK	Average cost per trainee	248	96	259	interactive video
Abbey National UK	Average cost per trainee	2,700	28	67	CBT

Source: adapted from Table 13.3 'Comparative costs per student of distance and traditional education systems' (Rumble, 1997)

Learners' aims

Vocational education and training courses provided for employees and other trainees can range from one-day workplace-based courses to three-year courses. In-company training provision is much more likely to be measured in days or weeks rather
than the months or years of the courses provided by the public sector through FE
Colleges, although this is changing as FE Colleges increasingly compete with
private providers for training contracts with companies. The length of a course does
not appear to be related to the approach adopted whether open, flexible, distance or
traditional. In our study, examples of long and short courses are found in all modes
(Table 3.4).

Table 3.4 *Units of measurement used to describe course length (OFL n= 238;
Traditional n= 264)*

Duration of course	OFL %	Traditional %
Days	20	31
Months	24	13
Years	48	51

Source: Calder *et al.* (1995)

In looking at training needs from the learners' perspective, there are four questions
which can be considered.

1. What are the aims of the learners? Why do they decide to undertake training?
2. How much choice do trainees currently have over the type of course and
    training which they undertake?
3. What features do they look for in training courses?
4. How do they find out about the options available to them?

Why trainees select the courses they do

As we have seen, there is considerable debate about the benefits or otherwise of
training for general versus specific development. In our own study, by far and away
the most common reason given for participating in vocational education and
training by the trainees, both employed and unemployed, was that it would help
their job prospects. In other words, it was not because it was primarily related to
their current job, but to the longer term – to general human capital development.
From the learners' point of view then, the courses they are involved in need to be
seen in terms of their relevance to themselves as individuals and to their future job
needs rather than just to their current jobs (see Table 3.5).

Table 3.5 *Reason for taking the course (OFL n= 238; Traditional n= 264)*

	OFL %	Traditional %
It will help my job prospects	84	80
I can go on to do further study	42	47
I can learn about things that interest me	39	44
It will help me develop as a person	32	45
Successful completion was necessary for my job	31	35

However, the skills needed for current jobs were seen as important. When respondents were limited to choosing just one main reason for why they were taking their course, the fact that successful completion was necessary for their current job came out as number two. There was no difference here between course participants on different types of course. Whether they were studying traditional courses or though OFL, general development was most important to individual learners, but specific development also played an important role in their participation in training activities.

Trainee choice

It has to be remembered that participation in training is not always a voluntary activity. This was brought home to us when we asked participants about the amount of choice they had had about whether to do the training. Although a majority of the people we studied (66 per cent OFL students and 57 per cent traditional course students) felt that it had been completely their own decision to undertake the training, this still left a substantial proportion for whom it was not.

Features trainees look for in training courses

In order to establish what factors were important to people in their choice of course, we asked participants in our study to rate those features which they felt to be very important to them personally. It emerged that the major factors were common to all participants regardless of their mode of study. Thus, the opportunity to get a good qualification was clearly seen as very important by almost half of the training participants. Similarly, the opportunity to develop, and the fact that the course should fit in with their job, were rated as very important by around 40 per cent or more of participants (Table 3.6).

However, there were three factors where clear and significant differences between participants studying in different modes did appear (Table 3.7).

Table 3.6 *Factors rated 'very important' in participants' choice of course*

Factors rated 'very important' in choice of course:	%
I can get a good qualification from the course	47
The course fits in with my job	41
The course offers the opportunity for me to develop...	40
The subject matter really interested me	38
I can work at my own pace★	24
I can learn at work	20
Flexibility of times of study★	18
Given my work responsibilities this is the only realistic option I had...	17
I wanted to try out something new	14
The starting date suited me	10
I can study at home	14
The flexible starting/finishing date suited me★...	13
Being able to take time out of study	12
Given my domestic responsibilities this is the only realistic option I had...	8
I had no option...	6

Note: ★significant difference between traditional and OFL students @ p = .0005

Table 3.7 *Factors affecting choice of course by study mode of participants (OFL n= 238; Traditional n= 264)*

	OFL %	Traditional %
I can work at my own pace	32	17
Flexibility of times of study	22	14
The flexible starting/finishing date suited me	17	9

An interesting feature of this particular set of factors is that, as we saw earlier, a substantial proportion of both traditional course and OFL course participants do like to learn at their own pace, and indeed there was no difference in the proportions who felt strongly about this between the two groups. The difference emerged when it comes to the point of actually choosing courses and the extent to which that factor actually played a part. The relative importance of the flexibility of the timing and duration of OFL courses for those who are studying through this mode bodes well given the anticipated growth of this type of course.

Finding out about the options available

Participants got their information about courses from a variety of sources. However, the importance of being in employment in order to get access to training is highlighted by the role of employers as the most important single source of information about training for many participants (see Table 3.8). However, friends and colleagues as well as tutors and teachers are also important sources for many participants.

Table 3.8 *Source of information about course (OFL n= 238; Traditional n= 264)*

First heard about course through	OFL %	Traditional %
employer	35	44
local newspaper	5	5
friend/colleague	18	11
teacher/tutor	16	18
parents/relative	1	3
other	16	14

These figures may well understate the importance of employers as a source of information about training for those actually in employment. Certainly, the Beinhart 1997 survey for the Department for Education and Employment suggests that over 80 per cent of those in employment studying courses related to their current job first heard about it in their workplace. However, for those studying with future job prospects in mind, employers as the first source of information slid down to a rather worrying 9 per cent (Beinhart and Smith, 1998).

Explanations of participation in education and training

Numerous research projects in Western Europe and in the US have sought to identify the factors which are key in adults' participation in formal education. Typologies of participation, motivational orientations, attrition and drop-outs abound. Briefly, the main models appear to be of three types (Woodley *et al.*, cited in (Harrison, 1993)) based on:

- motivation – explaining participation in terms of individuals achieving goals or identified needs
- sociology – explaining participation through the role of different groups in society, such as an outcome of social class with the school, for example, perpetuating disadvantage and inequality of opportunity
- supply-side models – explaining participation through the actions of institutions, such as the academic drift of academic institutions which are successful in access terms towards higher level and more exclusive roles.

Explanations from the learners' perspective inevitably give a different, and to some extent, more complex picture. In numerous studies, the reasons they identify for lack of participation in formal provision includes (adapted from Hillman, 1996):

- time
- child-care problems
- distance
- poor-quality information, and confusing and complex options and schemes
- admissions' policies which excluded potential learners
- negative past experience.

However, as has been stated, simple factors such as sources of information about courses can play an important role for different groups. While employers seem to be successful in getting information about courses to those learners who are already employed, and wish to take courses specifically linked to their current job, other groups appear to be reliant on a rather fragile network of informal and formal sources for their information. Younger learners, who have only recently left school or who still retain links with school, do still see it as a source of advice about further education and training. However, as those links attenuate, the outlook for the unemployed depends very much on the marketing skills of training providers themselves and of intermediaries such as Jobcentres.

The training providers

Basically, there appear to be four kinds of need which training providers attempt to meet (Table 3.9).

Table 3.9 *Four kinds of training need*

	Specific skills	Generic skills
Induction/preparation for job	1	3
Updating/improving performance	2	4

1. Induction and preparation of students and trainees for a specific job.
2. Updating or improving the performance of workers for a specific job.
3. Preparation of people for work through the acquisition of generic skills and knowledge.
4. Updating and improving people's performance in generic skills and knowledge.

Although both FE Colleges and in-company training departments are engaged in the provision of vocational education, there are some key differences as well as similarities in their overall aims and objectives.

1. Induction and preparation of students and trainees for a specific job

A major need identified by both FE tutors and course trainers on in-company courses was to prepare students and trainees for a specific job or to induct them into a specific job. Where induction courses are held frequently, and where companies operate on a multi-site basis, then open and flexible courses have been used with the benefits mentioned earlier. For example, they allow the same training to be offered to all new recruits by managers who are otherwise inexperienced in training and they allow induction training to be quickly updated. Of particular importance for national companies is the need to ensure that all staff in specific jobs acquire basic competencies to the same comparable national standard.

2. Updating or improving the performance of workers for a specific job

Improving an employee's performance in their job was clearly a major aim for courses in the in-company training sector. The use of regular staff appraisals by line managers appears to underpin the identification of training needs involving updating and upskilling. However, the need to update may be even more frequent than appraisal systems allow for. For example, new products, new or revised procedures and the introduction of new machinery will all carry with them the need to update the staff who are expected to handle goods, carry out correct procedures or operate new machines.

3. Preparation of people for work through the acquisition of generic skills and knowledge

Many of the aims identified by FE tutors were of the generic kind. In our study, tutors saw themselves as providing information and subject content, preparing students for work, encouraging students to take responsibility for their own learning, developing their skills as autonomous learners, teaching students to become more 'open-minded' and generally 'meeting students needs'.

4. Updating and improving people's performance in generic skills and knowledge

Finally, the aim of updating the knowledge and skills of personnel is clearly a crucial one for companies, and a number of the courses offered by both the FE and in-company training sectors were offered with this aim. Again, the courses run by the FE sector, such as Health and Safety in the Workplace, tended to be generic in content with the job 'personalization' occurring in part-time courses, through the application of the knowledge and skills gained by the student to their own workplace. The courses run by in-company training are usually specifically designed for the particular job held by the course participants.

The quality of the training provision

There does appear to be a crucial and quite key difference in the way in which public sector and in-company training providers assess the quality of their training. The assumption made by in-company providers was that the trainees would be successful in terms of acquiring the skills and knowledge being taught by the course. 'We train for success' was a comment made by trainers on different courses in different companies. Even where very specific technical skills or clearly identified competencies were being taught, the emphasis was on formative assessment, with the aim of ensuring that the trainees were trained to a specified standard within the shortest possible time. There was provision for some flexibility in recognition of the fact that people do learn at different speeds, but the failure of a course by a trainee was not a concept which had much relevance within in-company training.

In-company trainers then 'train for success'. Their task is to ensure that employees whom they are responsible for training acquire the skills and knowledge necessary for their job. The explanation for this situation appears to be rooted in the fact that even by just recruiting someone, before any induction and training has taken place, a company has undertaken a considerable investment. The training itself involves further investment by the company. Similarly with experienced staff, who are undertaking further training, say those who are being promoted to supervisory or first-line management positions, the amount of cumulative investment is considerable. So the employee who is to be trained is seen as someone who has already shown their suitability for training, by being selected for the job, or by being selected for promotion, or simply by virtue of holding a position, which requires training to cope with changes in the job. The task of the trainer is, therefore, to ensure that the employee acquires the knowledge, skills or competencies which have been identified as requirements for the job.

In contrast, the emphasis within FE Colleges is more on the individual learner and on the summative assessment of their performance. The modular nature of many courses now, together with the high proportion of formative assessment, which is now a feature of many courses, could be leading to a situation which more than nearly reflects that of in-company training. Nevertheless, the very different nature of the training provided by FE Colleges as compared with that provided through in-company training is, perhaps, partly an explanation for this difference. For example most of the FE College courses we included in our research lasted for at least one year, while some were two- or three-year courses. In contrast, the in-company training varied from a one-day full-time course up to those which lasted about six months part time.

Qualifications

Another major difference between public and in-company training providers is that while all the FE courses included in the study led to or were part of programmes which led to an external qualification, this was not the case with the in-company courses. Companies do, of course, often fund individuals who wish to study for a qualification, but these appear to be on courses which are organized and run by other providers. The overriding aim for FE tutors on courses for 16–18 year olds, for example, was frequently that their students should 'pass the exam and then move on either to further education or to employment'. However, some FE tutors did make the point that the acquisition of the qualification at which the course was aimed was often not the most useful measure of success for individual students. The example was given of particular jobs in the locality which had always been open to students with a 'D' grade GCSE in a particular subject. Therefore, local practice in what was seen as successful in this instance was different from the then Department of Education definition of 'C' grade or above as a success. Thus, the concept of 'value added' was instanced by some FE tutors as a preferred performance measure to the 'pass/fail' criteria.

Discussion

As mentioned previously, the Department of Employment has consistently promoted open learning as a cost-effective and timely approach for training purposes. Given the continuing pressure from the Funding Council for FE Colleges to reduce unit costs, open learning had inevitably been seen by many providers primarily as a way of cutting costs rather than as a way of improving learning. However, the cheapest route is not necessarily the most effective route in training as elsewhere.

Doyle argues that there are two fundamentally different types of competition, static and dynamic. Static competition 'takes the form of price, where low-cost companies grow at the expense of the less efficient. The social benefits of price competition are low inflation and incomes that buy more. To be an effective static competitor management must try to reduce costs below those of rivals... Dynamic competitors seek to win through innovation, by making their rivals' products obsolete. In contrast to static competitors, who are driven to reduce prices, the goal of dynamic competitors is to seek higher prices. They seek to do this by emphasising innovation and offering new products with superior features. Glaxo, Sony and Microsoft are examples' (Doyle, 1997).

Both types of competition are seen in the way the benefits of open learning are perceived by different stakeholders. So some training takes the cost reduction route, trying to provide the training which is seen as essential in the most efficient way possible, by reducing costs to the bone. Other providers take the 'dynamic' route whereby new training products are devised for which, it is argued, superior benefits accrue to the trainee and to the employer. Open, flexible and distance approaches to training can be used for either route. The one for which open and distance education is perhaps most well known is the provision of mass education and training at a low cost. However, the potential of telematics has meant that high cost but highly effective training programmes are also available. The problem then for businesses is whether to go the low cost route when buying in training, or to go the 'dynamic' route.

Employers' interest in open and distance approaches to vocational education and training is in the extent to which this type of training would enable them to achieve their primary goal, whether this was simple survival, profit maximization, growth or sector status. Certainly the interests of key decision-makers within companies and businesses may well be different, reflecting their varied responsibilities and areas of concern. However, there are two conflicting interpretations of the implications for the future of vocational education and training. One suggests that the primary concern is that there should be a flexible pool of low-grade workers willing to perform basic tasks at the lowest possible cost to the employer in order to maximize the competitiveness of the company. Examples which appear to support this view include (Boseley, 1994):

> ... the arrival of the flexible contract. The flexibility is for the employer, not the shop assistant or the shelf filler. The contract states that employees will be available for work as and when needed.
>
> Woolworths, Allied Maples and B&Q are among the companies using them. In the most extreme case, the zero hours contract, the company does not even guarentee to provide any work – but expects the worker to hold themselves ready for the call. The Burton Group, Kingfisher and the Store-house Group have introduced them.

The other interpretation (see Esping-Anderson, 1993, cited in Gooderham and Hines, 1995) suggests a shift from 'Fordist' to 'post-Fordist' methods of production with 'the hierarchical' organization being superceded by the 'flexible' organization, and the mass worker by the 'multi-skilled and autonomous worker'. However, the concern is that even under this scenario, a polarization would occur between the multi-skilled full-time worker and the non-core low-skilled part-time worker. The locus of responsibility for the training of these different groups is clearly different. Employers' interests vary with their type of business and their employee profile. For example, a company, which provides professional services, will have a very different staff profile and hence different sorts of training needs from a retail company or a major utility (Case Study 3.6).

The problem then in identifying the training needs, which must be met, is that there is a clear tension between the demands of companies operating within the two types of competitive markets. Employers' interest in human capital varies along with their interest in developing a stakeholder policy. Trainees and potential trainees need to acquire the skills needed for jobs now while recognizing that training is an investment in their own future. Training providers are increasingly needing to become multi-skilled in the knowledge and understanding of the options open to them in training contexts which can change only too rapidly.

The next chapter moves on to examine some examples of open and flexible solutions which have been devised to meet different types of training problem. The importance of not only examining the different components that make up a training course but of also organizing the sequencing and structure of the course to meet the learning capabilities of trainees is stressed. Learners' study skills vary considerably. Open, flexible and distance courses need to take account of learners' needs for help and support.

Case Study 3.6: Staff profiles and training needs – contrasting examples

Reuters

Reuters [over 14,000 employees globally in 1997], being essentially a knowledge-based organization, has a flat management structure and relatively few clerical or support staff. It consists predominantly of highly skilled and specialized staff...This group are also young – with a median age of 32. Being used to relatively high levels of responsibility, and the need for flexibility and initiative in their work, it is perhaps hardly surprising that they are also eager to take responsibility for their own learning...[1]

Severn Trent Water

Severn Trent is the second-largest of the ten privatized UK water companies... Its primary business is the supply of water and sewage treatment and disposal. It employs around 6,500 staff, with about 4,000 employed in white collar activities – clerical, administrative, supervisory, technical and management – and with about 2,500 craft and process manual workers.[2]

Sources: [1]Brown (1997)
[2]Calder and Newton (1995)

Chapter 4

Open, flexible and distance options

Introduction

Providers of vocational education and training which uses open, flexible and distance approaches have now built up considerable experience in their design and provision. Clearly open and flexible learning solutions to training problems vary considerably, as does their effectiveness. This section will examine in some detail the different courses and programmes using open, flexible and distance approaches, which have been designed and used by a range of different training providers.

Perceptions of OFL provision

The use of the terms 'open', 'distance' and 'flexible' can cause considerable confusion, even to those involved in education and training. This confusion is caused by the different ways in which people use the terms. In our study, tutors appeared to feel quite comfortable with the terms 'open and flexible learning', in spite of the variations in perceptions of what these terms meant. The term 'flexible', for example, was generally taken to refer to what one college called 'roll-on roll-off' courses. That is, courses that had some degree of flexibility about when the student might start, the duration of their studies and when they might complete. Open learning was sometimes taken to imply a choice of location of study for the student although, even here, the open learning workshops and Resource Centres operating within the companies and colleges did not necessarily allow students the choice of studying the materials at home.

The problems associated with the adoption and use of technical terms such as open and flexible education are not limited to professionals in the field. The terms are used increasingly in the training world in a variety of ways, but we wanted to establish what trainees and course participants understand by these terms. We, therefore, asked course participants in our study what their understanding of the terms were (Case Study 4.1).

Case Study 4.1: Students/trainees' perceptions of OFL provision

What students and trainees said the terms meant:

A traditional course is...

'learning in a classroom 5 days a week like at school' (FE student)
'full-time' (FE student)
'lecturer, students and books' (in-company trainee)
'set amount of work to get through' (in-company trainee)
'one where the tutor teaches, pupils copy, exams based on a classroom situation' (FE student)
'classroom-based – tutor/teacher "preaches" the course to students' (in-company trainee)

An open learning course is...

'open to anyone who wished to do the course without prerequisites' (FE student)
'one which allows work-based or home-based studying' (FE student)
'self-paced, self study, set times' (in-company trainee)
'given a chair and VDU and told to "work through the book"' (in-company trainee)
'correspondence' (FE student)
'a course done in the students own time at home, making use of tutors' (FE student)

A flexible course is...

'learning at your own pace' (FE)
'once per week' (FE)
'self-paced, self-study, no time limits' (in-company trainee)
'course can be constantly changed or is able to suit individual needs' (in-company trainee)
'a course which can be done at a leisurely pace with no fixed time limits for end exams' (FE)
'studying as and when time allows' (in-company trainee)
'fits in with your lifestyle' (in-company trainee)

Source: Calder *et al.* (1995)

As the examples above reveal, there are both interesting sets of agreements as well as diversities of opinion held among students and trainees as to what is meant by these terms. However, it is quite clear that there is a relative consensus that traditional courses are time-bound, location-bound, tutor-led and syllabus-bound.

In contrast there is a relative diversity of opinion about what an open learning course is. There are those who see it very much as independent learning while others see it as student-controlled, with tutors as a resource, which can be accessed when needed. There are clearly mixed views as to whether it is location-bound and in whose time the studying is done. Finally, the flexible courses appear to be seen as very student-centred. The general emphasis is on the pace and overall duration of the course rather than on the location of study. The control of the course by the student rather than by the tutor is implicit in these responses rather than explicitly stated.

Key design features in open and flexible courses

What also emerges from the reponses of the tutors and the course participants are a number of key features, which distinguish the different types of provision and which impact upon students' learning. This next section looks at a number of options selected and used by the training providers in our study. These are not intended as 'best practice' examples, but as illustrations of the range of options open to providers of vocational education and training who wish to use open, flexible or distance approaches (Table 4.1). You will notice that the principles of open access and open pedagogy in reality often play only a minor role in the design of provision, which is seen as using open and flexible methodologies.

Table 4.1 *Key design features in vocational education open learning courses*

Course design feature	Range of options
Access and participation	Open versus closed access Compulsory versus voluntary
Study setting	Home-based Work-based Special education/training premises
Curriculum	Tailor-made or off-the-peg
Media	Interactive versus passive media Single medium versus multiple media
Support	Tutor Mentor
Pacing and duration	Self-paced or externally directed
Assessment	Formative versus summative Reaching the required standard or competing with others?

Seven features that are key to the design of open, flexible or distance courses or programmes of study are identified. The decisions about each of these which need to be taken are discussed below.

Access and participation

Although the term 'open learning' is frequently used to indicate that access to learning is open to anyone who wishes or feels they might benefit from it, the reality is that access to most open learning is limited in some way. Open learning in relation to vocational education and training presents a particular challenge in trying to achieve openness of access.

Open versus closed access

The employer-provided training programmes which we studied were all closed access in that only employees of the appropriate status had entry to this training. Selection for participation was based on:

- appointment to a new job or to a new grade
- identified needs in staff appraisals
- individual staff request
- compliance with company policy

rather than on prior educational achievement. This is not to say that educational level did not play a part in the initial appointment or promotion of the staff member, but the trainers do not usually have much say in the selection of their trainees (Case Study 4.2).

Case Study 4.2: Post Office Counters Ltd

While Post Office Counters Ltd can and do select staff carefully – using aptitude tests during the recruitment stage – no such control is possible with the agency staff whom they train. Agency staff may be the owners of a small business which has taken on a sub-Post Office role, or they may be the employees of a large retailer which has decided to include Post Office facilities as a service to its customers.

Provision through the public sector has traditionally been relatively open access, although a common feature of the courses studied was the assessment of existing competencies or review of qualifications already held prior to enrolment for a course. Moves now being made by colleges towards market responsiveness is leading increasingly to the inclusion of provision, which is only open to specific corporate customers (Example 4.1).

Example 4.1: Hull College of FE: City and Guilds Process Plant Operations

The course is taught through open learning from materials developed and produced by Cleveland Open Learning Unit and bought through the Open College. The materials are still being modified in response to feedback from staff at Hull College. The course has been developed and is provided specifically for BP employees, with weekly support and tutorial sessions from staff from Hull College of FE, available at the BP Chemical Processing site on the edge of Hull.

The students on this course are a mixed age group (between about 19 and 50) with few if any educational qualifications. There are 15 students currently studying for Part 2. These are all BP employees. All potential students for this course have to apply both to their line manager and to the training section at BP for permission to do the course, as the cost of the course is met in part from the line managers budget and in part from the overall training budget. The college interviews each potential student using the full APEL procedure, and counsels them in considerable depth about the problems which studying through Open learning can present.

Source: Calder *et al.* (1995)

However, there are also examples of programmes which may be primarily intended for a particular corporate customer, but are nevertheless also open to other members of the public. For example, two similar courses in Personnel Practice offered by Plymouth College are offered in two different modes. The 'traditional' full-time block course is primarily for MOD personnel, but is open to others. The 'flexible' learning course which runs part time for nine months is more the traditional mix of trainees from different employers. The Department of Supervisory Management sees flexible courses as 'extending their hinterland'. Through offering a variety of modes of attendance and delivery they expand their market and widen access to their courses (Example 4.2).

Compulsory or voluntary participation?

Participation on training courses may be through choice, but is equally likely to be compulsory, either as a condition of employment or as a condition for receiving benefit. Participation in employer-provided training for basic grade staff is usually compulsory for the selected employees, for example:

- new staff – induction training (compulsory attendance)
- selected existing staff – updating or upgrading of skills (compulsory attendance).

Example 4.2: Plymouth College of FE: Personnel Practice and Safety and Health (within the Department of Supervisory Management)

The supervisory management department specializes in part-time courses and flexible provision. Courses can be designed to meet individual customer requirements in terms of price, content, location, delivery and technique.

The staff within the department have not travelled the traditional route into education, having strong business backgrounds and awareness.

The department runs a lot of resettlement programmes for the MOD. One of the block courses on offer is a five week full-time college attendance programme where they get a general management qualification plus a specific qualification relating to a functional area of management, for example personnel practice. The majority of people on the block courses are MOD but there are some people from local firms and unemployed people. These programmes are run once a term, so there are usually three in an academic year.

In the flexible course, for personnel at a junior level, the nine month work programme is designed around the workplace, for example the workbooks are completed around and in relation to their work practices. Also there is a mentoring scheme whereby an individual within the company (usually the line manager) acts a a support and mentor to the student within the organization, and also provides feedback to the college

Source: Calder *et al.* (1995)

Unemployed trainees equally may have to participate in recognized vocational training courses in order to meet criteria for receiving benefit. So, whereas in-company training courses are likely to include people who are there for similar reasons, participants in courses offered by other providers are likely to be more diverse in their circumstances and in their motivation.

Study setting

The major large-scale providers of open and flexible learning in the UK have on the whole focused on learners who would be studying in their own homes. However, with traditional forms of vocational education, the training was designed to take place primarily in the workplace and at college, with the trainee or apprentice being expected to supplement this with homework. The tradition of work-related training taking place during working hours still seems to predominate for all training except those for which qualifications are awarded. In our study, all the shorter courses – those of two or three days duration – were undertaken in work time and were based either at work or at special training premises. Some of the longer courses did have elements that could have been home-based, but both the trainers and the trainees expected the work to be undertaken in work time. The use of more experienced or senior staff as mentors also has a bearing on the matter of study location as they can only operate in a work-based setting (Table 4.2).

Table 4.2 *Study settings and support options*

	Individual	Tutor	Mentor	Group
Home-based	✓	X	X	X
Residential	✓	✓	X	✓
Work-based	✓	✓	✓	✓
Education/training premises	✓	✓	X	✓

The question of location of study or study-setting has become increasingly complex with the use of open, flexible and distance methods. For example where tutors are used, then the setting is normally one which allows for a number of students to meet with or to talk to the tutor such as residential settings, work premises or education or other training premises. Where mentors are used, then the training setting will be on work premises; and where group learning or a group activity is part of the process, then again, home-based settings are ruled out. Home-based study is, therefore, really only feasible for individual study sessions. Similarly, although we found examples of tutors providing training in three of the four main settings for training, the problem for course providers was one of making time available during working hours and of finding an appropriate location at work.

The study-setting options for unemployed trainees were more limited. The growth of competence-based courses such as NVQs does mean that relevant work experience of some sort is often essential. Providers had either to set up simulations at the college or on training premises, or arrange a training attachment. However, while appropriate work placements may sometimes be difficult for colleges to arrange, employers may experience similar problems in arranging study facilities for their own staff (Case Study 4.3).

Curriculum

Tailor-made or off-the-peg

We have seen that one of the most difficult questions with which providers have to grapple is the extent to which they should focus only on the provision of training which is specific to their needs, or widen the provision out to include more general training. Major monopolies such as Post Office Counters or the Inland Revenue clearly have training needs which, in terms of content, are unique to those organizations. In contrast,

Example 4.3: Inland Revenue

Staff are expected to organize their own work time so that they can work through the course materials, get the reading done and the information for the work-based problems. However the tutors spoken to felt that there were real problems with this in that offices were so busy. Even holding live tutorial sessions in the workplace was seen as problematic because of the many distractions.

'… When they come to do the material, if they're doing it at their desk with the telephone ringing, if they haven't got any discipline or if they're expected to answer the phone, then the effectiveness plummets' (tutor).

Source: Calder, McCollum *et al.* (1995)

supermarkets share the majority of their training needs with numerous other employers. However, even where the training is general in content, the open learning training package used may still be designed specifically for that employer (Table 4.3).

Table 4.3 *Tailor-made or off-the-peg provision*

Course package	Company-specific content	General content
Sole user	✓	✓
Many users	X	✓

This situation is not limited to private providers. There are many examples of FE College tutors who prefer to design and produce their own open learning materials for students studying for a nationally recognized qualification. The reasons for this can vary from lack of knowledge about how best to go about finding and assessing the quality of published training packages in a particular training topic to wishing to incorporate and emphasize aspects of the curriculum, which are different from those covered by known packages. Tutors who have not previously been involved with open and flexible learning may not necessarily know about key sources of information such as the ICDL national database of open learning courses, or the NEC range of courses.

Media

Range of media we found

The modern technologies that grab the headlines are in no way typical of the range of media used in the vast majority of open and distance programmes used for basic level vocational education and training. While universities experiment with leading edge technology, and major multinationals introduce high-tech programmes for key specialist and management staff, the vast majority of open and distance vocational training applications use technologies which are accessible, simple and straightforward to prepare and to use. What might be called 'appropriate technology' rather than high technology. For example, part of the material which trainees used during their induction period with Safeway were small pocket-sized cards with details of the key competencies they were working on. The card was designed to fit into their overall pocket for convenience so that they (and their mentors) could easily glance at it during the working day.

The media which may be used are usually text, video- or computer-based. Audio did not feature as a normal option in the courses which we examined, although its success in some countries as a teaching medium is well documented. Two aspects in particular emerged as important: firstly, the extent to which the media used to get the learner actively involved in *doing* rather than just in *taking in* information and advice and secondly, the extent to which they are the sole media used on a course, or whether a selection of different media are used.

Interactive provision

The term 'interactive media' is increasingly used as shorthand for computer-aided instruction. However, this limits unnecessarily the ways in which different media can be designed to interact with a learner. Laurillard (1993) suggests that media may be claimed to operate 'interactively' when 'the students can act to achieve the task goal'. She continues, 'they should receive meaningful intrinsic feedback on their actions that relate to the nature of the task goal; something in the "world" must change as a result of their actions'.

Thus, texts, for example, need to have not only questions, exercises and activities included, but they need answers, together with detailed explanations of those answers. In our study, considerable frustration was reported by learners using open learning texts who, if they were unable to satisfactorily answer an in-text question, were then simply referred back to particular parts of the original text. Rowntree's concept of a 'tutorial in print' is useful here. If a learner, by his answer, shows that he has not grasped the principle which is being taught, the tutor will follow through with alternative explanations and questions. The open learning text attempts to provide a similar role in print (Lockwood, 1992).

Single medium versus multiple media

Although course designers do try to incorporate the media that are most likely to achieve the best learning result, much open and flexible learning does still rely exclusively on print-based media with a variety of face-to-face support. However, there are many examples of more than one type of media being used in open and flexible courses for vocational education and training. Ideally, the appropriate media would always be selected on the basis of the teaching task being undertaken. So, if students were learning how to handle different sorts of interaction between two people, body language as well as dialogue would be important, and a video sequence would be one way of ensuring that the appropriate aspects were both seen and heard. Similarly, the initial stages of some manual skill might more safely or cheaply be taught through computer simulation than in a real life situation. Complex procedures on machine maintenance might be taught through interactive video. British Telecom for example has well-documented examples of using CBT and interactive video in their training, although, as this report shows, assumptions about the ways in which 'non-management' grades learn can have a limiting effect on choice of media and the structure of the learning package (Case Study 4.4).

Case Study 4.4: British Telecom

The medium of interactive video helped to distinguish the product in the minds of the target audience from the kinds of CBT used by the non-management grades... The underlying model of learner behaviour was quite different from the philosophy applied to technical training. The prevailing view in technical training was that technical grades needed to be told what they should learn, then taught it in a straightforward, didactic way, then tested on their recall and understanding and either passed as competent, or referred back for revision. The management training philosophy was that managers were responsible for their own development needs; were capable of making judgements about what they needed to learn, when, how much and at what pace. Management training was therefore much better suited to an open or distance learning approach, whereas technical training was modelled more on a programmed learning approach.

Source: Brown (1997)

However, constraints such as access to the appropriate media, portability, place of study, cost, technical competence and lead-in time all combine to limit the number and type of media through which training is offered. Simplicity in the design of a course is also of benefit where the support available to trainees may be untrained in the use of different instructional media.

Support

The issue of support is seen as an essential element in the provision of open learning – in particular personal support for learners. Indeed, many see the provision of appropriate and timely support as the key feature that distinguishes open learning from independent learning using learning packages. Although in the literature there are many case studies of courses that use telephone support and, increasingly, support using computer mediated communication (CMC), this type of provision does not yet appear to be in much use for training at basic technician and craft levels. Personal support for students and trainees on the open and flexible learning courses which we investigated was normally provided by either tutors or mentors, mentors usually being the trainees' supervisors or line managers. This support may be either on a one-to-one basis or in groups.

Face-to-face support from tutor

The way in which tutors are used does vary considerably. The providers we spoke with had developed a whole variety of different ways of using a scarce and expensive resource to maximum effect with students and trainees. Learners views about the type and extent of support they need vary almost as much as the learners themselves.

> The tutors are very important, after a certain level you get stuck, the tutors are there for when you get stuck, you could not manage without the tutors (FE part-time open learning GCSE student).

The importance of the tutor as a motivator was a message which came out strongly from the FE sector providers. This was particularly the case with course packages which replicated traditionally taught courses. The amount of tutor input matched, and in some cases exceeded the tutor time normally available in traditional tutor-led courses (Example 4.3).

Example 4.3: Plymouth College of FE: GCSE Maths Flexistudy Workshop

The tutor role was viewed as a key role in the learning process and quite distinctive from a teacher's role in a traditional class. The tutor role was to help and to explain things on a one to one basis and also to keep an eye on students' progress. There was always a tutor on duty in the Maths Workshop, during the set hours, and students worked individually through their booklets. The tutor role was viewed as critical in terms of encouraging and motivating the students, particularly at the beginning of term when students were unused to flexible learning. The majority of students doing the GCSE are in the 16–18 age range, coming straight from school, and the key problem for the students, as perceived by the tutors was one of motivation and self-discipline. One of the main disadvantages of flexible provision centred around this issue, and the flexible learning process was therefore viewed as much more suited for mature and self-disciplined students. As one tutor said 'for those that are motivated it's an excellent system'.

Source: Calder *et al.* (1995)

Tutor support was mainly provided through face-to-face support, although we came across instances of tutors giving their phone numbers to students on externally assessed courses for use in an emergency. We also came across both one-to-one and one-to-many tutor options. Examples of one-to-one options included:

- limited but regular availability on site at set hours in a set room to both individual trainees for queries and to groups for lectures and seminars (BP course at Hull)
- at college on a weekly basis for set hours in a personal tutorial role (Rochdale)
- sustained availability for a very limited period – on-site – to explain and introduce trainee to basic systems and procedures (Post Office Counters) (Case Study 4.5).

One-to-many tutor options included:

- intensive workshops in a residential setting to supplement trainees' earlier study of video and text materials (Post Office machines (Case Study 4.6), Inland Revenue)
- residential courses for groups – traditional role (Inland Revenue)
- workplace-based courses for groups for induction and for updating – traditional role (Inland Revenue and Post Office Counters)
- instant availability for individuals on request in regular group-based work-shop – explain and help individuals with specific problems (Plymouth College of FE).

Case Study 4.5: Post Office Counters Ltd: Own and agency staff training

Post Office Counter training for agency staff - The course for agency staff uses one to one coaching for up to 2 weeks, supplemented in parallel by workbooks. The tutor comes back for two further periods of a half day to deal with any problems and identify any errors which may be being made. Again, the booklets are made available for use and further reference during this period. Tutors are former counter staff who have been trained to TDLB standards. Line managers are seen as having a training role which is exercised through the staff appraisal programme.

Tutor role: The training is designed to give the tutor a central role, with the tutor determining which materials the trainee needs and when they need it. The very high cost of the one to one training which is necessary for agency staff means that open learning has to carry much of the reinforcement role. The activities and self-contained exercises within the materials are designed to replicate as far as possible all the paperwork and documentation with which counter staff are expected to be familiar.

Source: Calder *et al.* (1995)

Case Study 4.6: Post Office Technical and Engineering Branch: Culler Facer Cancellor Course

Culler Facer Cancellor Course – an Open Learning course involving 16-20 hrs of personal study plus a one and a half week residential course. This course is designed for sorting machine operators who will have to operate the CFC sorting machine. A package of text materials, video and activities are sent to the trainee for study prior to the residential component of the course. Tutors tend to see themselves as providing skills training. This involves an emphasis on practical handling of machines and constant assessment of trainees' understanding and retention of the information and skills they are being taught in order to carry out the required tasks. The courses are tightly geared to ensuring that everyone as far as possible reaches at least the minimum level of competence on all key tasks.

Tutor role: The tutor's role is seen as central to the training. The preparatory open learning package is seen as a way of maximizing the benefit that trainees get from the work-shop component. The tutors see their task as training as many staff as possible to the required standards within the overall time allowed. For example, if ten new machines a month are arriving at sites around the country and there is only twelve months in which to train up all the staff, then tutors recognize that the timescale is only feasible by minimizing the amount of time trainees need to spend at the residential workshop.

Tutor role: The tutors start with the assessment of students to establish existing competencies. They also visit students' workplaces and monitor students' progress, the assessment of the student by the work supervisor and to deal with any problems. For the Business Administration course, each student has a 'monthly review' to assess their progress on a more formal basis, and this is recorded on their Action Plan. Both short and long-term goals are reviewed at each session.

'It takes very different skills teaching one to one and group. The techniques you use and whatever are different.'

Source: Calder *et al.* (1995)

Face-to-face support from mentor

Mentor support is used extensively to support trainees during periods of work-based training. The supervisors and line managers who act as mentors may or may not have received any special training for that role (Case Study 4.7 and Example 4.4). Their advantages are:

- sustained availability over a long period on site, linked to the company training manager who will have general oversight of trainee's progress
- sustained availability on site linked to tutor at college who will have general oversight of trainee's progress

Case Study 4.7: Safeway: Headstart Training Programme

Trainees have a 2 day group induction which is carried out by a senior manager from the store using a detailed 'Tutor Induction Guide'. They then go over to department managers for on-the-job training which consists of working through a series of workbooks which detail the competencies to be acquired. The headstart programme lasts for 12 weeks, and they have a monthly review, and a weekly review with their department manager to discuss progress.

Training role for everyone: In each of the training programmes, supervisory staff have a key role to play as mentors to those undertaking training, and in carrying out this role they are supported by and dependent upon very carefully structured learning materials for assessing the acquisition of competencies.

Source: Calder *et al.* (1995)

Example 4.4: Plymouth College of FE – Certificate in Personnel Practice

Examining Body: Institute of Personnel Management (IPM)

Course Aims: To provide a practical understanding of specific personnel management techniques.

Course Content: Interactive skills, personnel practice, recruitment and selection, training and development, employee relations.

Course format and duration: Modules are based on workshops of 2–4 days duration over a 9 month period or as a 5 week full-time block release course.

The Certificate has two very distinct sets of customers, the block course for service people which runs for 5 weeks and the flexible learning which is for personnel at a junior level, and runs for 9 months. Thus whilst 'you're talking theoretically the same level, the customer is very different'.

Whilst the course content is virtually identical in both sets of courses there are significant differences in approaches to the subject. In the flexible course the work programme is designed around the work place, for example the work books are completed around and in relation to their work practices. Also there is a mentoring scheme whereby an individual in the company (usually the line manager) acts as a support and mentor to the student within the organization, and also provides feedback to the college. There is a mentor training session run by the college, but the response here is variable.

The training function is brought into everyone's job, that's deliberate, the department manager is responsible for training staff, training is built into competency (Safeway manager).

I found that without giving guidance and support and encouragement they don't use the new skills, but if I give support then they're enthusiastic and they use their skills, its a knock on effect (Safeway departmental manager).

Pacing and duration

Comments have already been made on the tremendous variation in the duration of vocational education courses, ranging as they do from a few days to years of study. With the flexibility in pacing offered by many open and flexible courses, this variation in duration can affect trainees even on the same course. There are limits, however, to the amount of flexibility which is feasible within a course or set of courses. Flexible education and training courses offered by FE Colleges tend to last for periods of six months to a year. In part, this is related to the traditional academic year and to the fact that the majority of students are following courses from which they expect to get some form of qualification. In contrast, the courses available through in-company training which we came across ranged from a single day to (exceptionally for basic grade courses) six months. Typically, where no external qualification is involved, in-company courses at basic craft and service levels appear to be designed on the basis of 3–5 days full time equivalent.

Self-paced

The facility to work at your own pace was one of the key features which the learners themselves associated with open and flexible learning and which they valued. While many of the courses we came across do allow trainees this freedom, the reality is that the constraints of vocational training programmes often mean that self-pacing is not a real option except where extra time is needed for particular individuals to reach the desired standard. In particular, where students and trainees are registered for a course which leads to an external qualification, tutors are only too concerned that self-pacing might mean no pace at all (Examples 4.5 and 4.6).

It would be a mistake, however, to assume that tutors were unsympathetic to the idea of self-pacing. Even within the same institution a range of views can exist on the desirability of this feature of open and flexible provision.

the old system, before we had flexible learning, was designed to suit the staff. Students had a set amount of time allocated to each piece of work – this was easy for the staff, but for the slower students, they never managed to complete fully some of the more demanding pieces of work (FE tutor).

Example 4.5: Hull College of FE – Process Plant Operations: City and Guilds

In the past, before counselling was introduced, 20 to 30 per cent of students never completed their first module. The college feels that the biggest problem for students with Open Learning is self-discipline. They therefore feel it is helpful for the students if they are put under some form of duress by the employer (who is also the sponsor) for deadlines. At BP, a strict regime is operated. If the college is concerned about lack of progress, a letter is sent to the BP training department who then call the student in. There may also be pressure from the line manager. If lack of progress continues, the student may end up having to pay for their own materials.

Example 4.6: North Devon College Department of Technology (Construction Section)

Flexible learning allows students greater autonomy and responsibility in their learning, however, with some students and tutors this poses a degree of contradiction. There seemed to be a view that some students had to be 'pushed along', as this follows what they had experienced at school, and that if the teacher did not 'drive' students they would waste their time. This issue of motivation may well be a real difficulty with some of the students.

Competency-based training in the workplace, however, does seem to enable self-pacing to be more of a reality. Even here, if a group of employees is being supported by trainers external to the company, there may be pressures on individuals to complete within a set period of time. Set assessment dates, residential components and periods of group tuition all nibble away at the opportunity for trainees to be self-pacing. The reality is that there can be relative freedom to slow down or to speed up on occasions, but that externally imposed key dates and deadlines make genuine self-pacing in vocational training courses a relative rarity.

Assessment

The task of the trainer in vocational education is to ensure that the employee or learner acquires the knowledge, skills or competencies which have been identified as needed for the job, be it a current job or some future job. The opening up of access to vocational education and training by removing many of the barriers of entry qualifications, age limits, and course attendance regulations has brought with it increasing concerns among stakeholders about how best to ensure comparability of standards of training across sites within the same company, and across different types of training providers for the same qualifications. For example, line managers can be used to assess the skills and knowledge acquisition of those of their staff under training. This is achieved through the use of records of specified compe-tences. Ideally, such staff should be trained in assessment and verification to set standards, but unless the managers have themselves been trained and accredited for standards assessment and verification, the issue of assuring common standards across different managers and across different sites does present considerable problems.

The two major forms of assessment used in vocational education and training are:

- assessment which is essentially geared to identifying the areas in which a trainee could benefit from additional help and support (formative assessment)
- assessment which is geared to identifying the standard of knowledge, skill or understanding which a trainee has reached (summative assessment).

The timing of assessments is an entirely separate issue. Assessment can take place at the end of the course, or it can take place at different points throughout training. For example, both formative and summative assessment can take place at different stages during the course. Continuous assessment is increasingly popular both because it can be used for formative purposes early enough in the training to enable the tutor to modify the help being given to the trainee, and because, if it is used for summative purposes (as in many modular courses), then it takes the pressure of 'all or nothing' exams off students' shoulders.

Formative versus summative

The majority of the in-company training which we saw had no formal assessment of trainees as such. Although competency-based training clearly does use summa-tive assessment, the reality is that individuals in training, who have not acquired the particular competence being assessed, then work further at it until they have reached an acceptable minimum standard. Getting staff up to the required standard is very much seen as the tutor's task (or the mentor's reponsibility where they are used), rather than the responsibility of the individual trainee.

Because FE Colleges are more likely to be preparing students for public exams, they tend to operate formal assessment procedures which might be internally assessed, externally assessed, or some combination of the two. However, increased provision of company-based training by FE Colleges means that student perform-ance is no longer necessarily assessed on some courses (Example 4.7).

Example 4.7: Post Office

Assessment was important on these courses. On the up-dating courses, formal assessment was built into the residential component. On the induction courses, the assessment was more informal, but neverthelss a common minimum level of competency had to be achieved. There was flexibility in the open learning version of the induction courses for counter work to extend the training period if the tutor felt it to be necessary.

Source: Calder *et al.* (1995)

Plymouth College of FE: National Certificate in Occupational Safety and Health

Assessment procedures are very similar whether for the 5 week block course or the [nine month part-time] distance course. There is a practical where students go into a workplace and write a management report on their observations which the tutor assesses on behalf of Nebosh and exams are set and marked by Nebosh. However during the [five week full-time course] there is less time and opportunity to do individual assessments.

Source: Calder *et al.* (1995)

Reaching a required standard or competing with others?

One reason for the continuing difference in attitude to assessment between public provision of vocational education and in-company provision is that in-company training is specifically designed to enable trainees to achieve a given standard of competence, so it is quite usual, if selection for the course has been carried out well, for there to be no one who fails to achieve the given standard. In contrast, many external qualifications, such as the GCSE, are achieved in competition with other candidates and there will always be losers, no matter how good the range of candidates is. The growth of the national competency-based NVQ system of assessment is beginning to make inroads here, but with concerns about the amount of bureaucracy which can be involved. Some employers are expressing concerns that the lower level qualifications are based only on what trainees can do rather than on what they know or understand. It is difficult to make predictions about future likely trends.

Putting the pieces together

The extent to which a learner already possesses the study skills necessary for independent learning clearly makes a difference in terms of the way a course needs to be structured. The type and amount of support a learner needs, the type and frequency of assessment procedures and feedback, the detail in which learning goals are specified, the amount of 'redundancy' in the materials, guidance on pacing and on key milestones are all aspects of the design of a course where individual learners' needs will vary in relation to how skilled they are already at learning – in other words, how self-directed they are (Example 4.8).

Example 4.8: North Devon College: Department of Food and Fashion – Hotel and Catering courses

Students study skills, their capability for independent study and their overall motivation are all issues which come into prominence with OFL. There was a view amongst some of the tutors interviewed that many of the students did not have the necessary study skills and had not developed sufficiently as learners for them to meet some of the demands of OFL. For example, many students had problems with sufficient levels of core skills and literacy, which meant that they had considerable difficulty with some of the self-instructional open learning texts. Some tutors who taught the core science modules, also had to use these sessions for developing basic study skills. Another aspect of the basic skills, mentioned by a number of tutors was 'students need good organization skills' for keeping check on their studies, as they progress towards submitting themselves for the competency assessments. Although 'organizational skill' seems to be a requirement for students to gain maximum benefit from OFL, it appears that many of them have not yet developed sufficiently in this way. With the commitment of the staff students are supported in developing their study skills. However, helping students with these skills creates extra demands for the teaching staff. It was felt that some of the students had been systematically failed through the school system and had been told that 'catering is the only thing you can do' by their school. This problem was compounded by the generally low status in which the catering profession is viewed throughout the whole culture of the region. Given the backgrounds of some of the students, it is not surprising that they are not sufficiently developed and lack the skill needed for independent study.

Source: Morgan (1995)

Hull College of FE

There was a shared perception among tutors across the different courses that school leavers needed additional help, support and encouragement to avoid the danger of drop-out. However it was also felt that thorough counselling prior to starting the course helped to prepare students... The benefits to students of studying through OFL which tutors identified included preparation for lifelong learning and greater flexibility for meeting individual learning needs in relation to pace of study, with people able either to accelerate their studies or slow them down.

Source: Calder *et al.* (1995)

Even within so-called traditional training provision, learners' experiences can vary dramatically from course to course. On one course the tutor may adopt a didactic approach, using whole class teaching, regular formative assessment with an end of course summative assessment. On another course, the tutor may use videos to stimulate discussion, small group project work, student-led tutorials, practicals using simulated work situations, and a mix of formative and continuous summative assessment. When moving into the area of opportunities presented by open and flexible learning, the constraints of entry qualifications, time, place and duration of study may all disappear – it depends on the course characteristics. It is the way the different components are put together, however, which can make a huge difference to the effectiveness of a course using open and flexible methods.

Over the past 20 years or so, a large number of different types of open learning courses have been generated to meet the needs of different stakeholders. Leach and Webb have listed five examples of programmes with direct relevance for technician and craft level education and training. The models they describe offer some insight into the sort of open learning which a major provider such as the NEC initiates and supports (Example 4.9).

Example 4.9: Five models of open learning for vocational education and training

1. NEC Technician Training Scheme: Students study materials over an academic year. They attend college on three or four occasions for tutorial support and assessment. Predominantly used for small numbers of employees. Success on the course is tied to career progression.

2. Main system: Basically distance teaching, using learning materials structured to include study guidance, revision guidance, and advice on pacing. The modular structure allows for gaps in study, and changes to assignment deadlines. Telephone contact is encouraged.

3. ABACUS: A mix of home-based study and face-to-face workshops on a monthly basis. Units are linked to NVQ competences. Simulation of work situations is used, rather than real work-based experience.

4. Flexistudy: A combination of distance and face-to face study. Students receive materials by post for home-based study. They send or take their assignments to local FE colleges for marking, feedback on assignments, and sometimes for tutorial support.

5. Open Learnng Units: Students select open learning material from the college-based OLU and negotiate a learning programme with their tutor.

Source: Leach and Webb (1993)

What these models do not give details of, however, is the balance and sequencing of the different media and types of support. The importance of such aspects becomes apparent when we look in more detail at some of the examples from our study.

Models of provision being operated

We will focus on just six examples, selected to highlight the different types of provision offered through open, flexible and distance modes:

1. GCSE Maths Workshop at Plymouth FE College
2. 'headstart' initial training for retail staff at Safeway Foodstores
3. new supervisors course at the Inland Revenue
4. initial counter training for agency staff by the Post Office
5. in-service courses for employees by Rank Xerox.

By looking at each example in terms of the sequencing and balance of the different course components, we can develop a way of looking at each type of course as a whole, rather than simply in terms of its parts. It is in the mixing and sequencing of the course elements that the different models can be seen.

1. The classic 'open' model

The first model – from the Maths GCSE Workshop example from Plymouth – represents what is probably the most common model; or at least the one which appears to most clearly reflect the common perception of what is meant by open learning (Example 4.10).

Example 4.10: GCSE Maths Workshop (Plymouth FE College)

This course was a one- to two-year course designed primarily for youngsters retaking GCSE. Core teaching was through a series of short specially designed workbooks which included self-assessment exercises. Students worked through the workbooks individually and at their own pace during timetabled sessions. A tutor was available during each session if the student wanted advice or help. Overall monitoring of progress of individual students was carried out by the tutor. Summative assessment was through the public examination system.

The learning comprises a media-led core, which can be studied at the student's own pace, with regular tutorial support available. The workshop is different from any of the models described by Leach and Webb in that student learning is primarily college-based, and a tutor is available at all times to provide any advice or help needed by the student. The strength of this model is that support is available as and when the student needs it. The weakness is that study takes place at fixed times, and in a fixed location

2. Two-phase initial group model

This model occurred on several occasions. Basically, it consists of two phases: an initial group phase followed by individual workplace-based training supported by specially designed materials. The initial group induction may be led by a trained tutor (as in the counter training course) or by a member of senior staff using detailed support materials (as with the headstart training model). This is then followed by further training in a work location supervised by line managers acting as mentors (Example 4.11).

Example 4.11: 'Headstart' initial training for retail staff (Safeway Foodstores)

The 'headstart' training is provided for all non-managerial full-time retail staff on their recruitment by the company. All staff prior to entry are assessed via a short 'test' which supplements their job interview. After recruitment, the core teaching takes place in two phases. Phase 1 is the two-day group induction which is carried out by a senior manager from the store using a detailed 'Tutor Induction Guide'. Phase 2 continues over a period of approximately three months and consists of working through a series of workbooks which detail the competencies to be acquired. Core training, therefore, takes place through work activities overseen by a supervisor who acts as 'mentor'. Supervision and competency assessment is exercised by supervisors. On satisfactory completion of all the required competencies, staff receive an increase in their wages.

The advantages of this particular structure are that because both tutor and group support is available during the first part of the training, learner confidence can be established, together with an understanding of the training approach being used and the expectations of them as learners can be made clear. The subsequent training in the workplace enables them to grow in confidence in their own ability to acquire the necessary competence and to become more 'independent' as learners. The disadvantages of this approach are that learners only get a fixed length initial induction, and may still need considerable guidance from their mentors during the early stages of their workplace training

3. 'Club sandwich'

Several courses in our study were found to be running training courses with this particular structure. Basically, it consists of alternating periods of residential training and independent distance learning. The principle on which this model is based is that the 'difficult' aspects of the course, which include detailed information which has to be memorized and understood, are presented in text form and are sent to participants to be studied prior to each residential phase. This should, in principle, leave time for the activities undertaken during the residential phases to concentrate on practising the application of that knowledge and on any interpersonal components of the course (Example 4.12).

Example 4.12: New supervisors' course (Inland Revenue)

This course is for staff new to the role of supervisor within the Inland Revenue. It, therefore, includes both new staff freshly recruited to the service, and existing staff who have been promoted. The course is designed to be completed over a period of six months in three phases. Core teaching is perceived as being provided by three sets of week-long residential group training, with a series of six booklets which hold essential knowledge being sent to individuals to study as preparation for each residential phase. There is no formal assessment associated with the course.

The advantages of this approach are primarily ones of cost. Residential provision is expensive, so by pulling out the personal study aspects represented by the information which staff are expected to memorize and understand, the time spent on the expensive component can be minimized. The disadvantages of this approach are that it takes no account of the way in which people learn, nor of how they are motivated. By putting the study of the reading materials before the residential component, assumptions are being made about the learning skills possessed by the trainees. Unless the materials used are of very high quality, and unless staff are motivated to undertake the necessary preparatory work, the sorts of problem reported for courses structured in this way are likely to keep recurring. Namely, that staff don't undertake the preparatory work before attending the residential course, leading to the need for tutors to cover the ground anyway during the residential component.

4. Progressive attenuation

This model starts off with high support both from a tutor and from specially designed support materials. This support is decreased as the trainee acquires confidence and competence (Example 4.13).

The advantages of this structure are that the tutor can modify the initial induction to meet the individual trainee's particular needs and level of learning skills in the most appropriate and effective way for that trainee. The continuing availability of support if needed, during the subsequent period, provides an important safety net for the trainee. The disadvantages relate primarily to the switch from highly supported learning to having to rely on materials for information. The degree of success achieved by this approach will depend on the flexibility retained by the tutor for moving from high levels of support to much lower levels of support, and how comfortable trainees feel in using the support materials.

Example 4.13: Initial counter training for agency staff (Post Office)

This course is designed for people who buy or are employed by a Post Office Counter franchise as part of another retail business. Thus, owners of small village shops, employees of large stores which operate a Post Office counter as part of their service to customers, and the like, all need training in the operation of Post Office Counter services. The training parallels the aims of the course provided for the Post Office Counter's own staff. The core teaching for the agency course comprises an intensive one-to-one teaching in the work setting over a period of one to two weeks. This is followed by a further period of up to two weeks using specially designed workbooks including self-assessment material and materials for simulation exercises during which time the trainee is operating alone at the counter. These workbooks are used as an adjunct to and to supplement the work with the tutor. The tutor is on call during this period should there be any problems. There is no formal summative assessment although the tutor is responsible for determining the competency of the trainee.

---

5. Independent learning using a distance package

This model is in widespread use. Represented here by the Rank Xerox in-service staff development and updating approach – this model operates on the principle of, wherever possible, leaving the choice of mode to the student. Thus, the trainee can choose whatever study mode is personally convenient and acceptable. These types of course are usually only of about one or two days length for 'live' courses, or between five and twelve hours of independent study time.

Example 4.14: In-service courses for employees (Rank Xerox)

All full-time employees have an average of 40 hours' personal development training every year. A range of training topics such as technical training, project control, appraising, time management and so on are available to staff. Many courses are available either as 'live' courses for groups of staff, or as an 'open learning' option. The 'open learning' option is actually a self-contained pack which may be video, text, CD-ROM or mixed media. No formal tutorial support is offered. The choice of mode remains with the member of staff. There is no formal summative assessment.

The main advantage of this approach is that the learner is in control and can choose the mode which is most convenient and with which they are most comfortable. The main disadvantage is that there is no opportunity to develop independent learning skills through supported open learning.

Discussion

Even from the few examples given here it will be clear that the number of ways in which components can be combined to provide vocational education and training are limited only by providers' imaginations. In comparing these different models, what becomes apparent is the very different assumptions being made by the course designers about the level of trainee learning dependency which they are catering for. The term dependency is used here in the sense of the ability of the learner or trainee to be self-directed. The support needs of adults and their need for direction from a teacher do vary considerably; in other words, their need for the relevance and the usefulness of the goals of the training to be clarified and for their confidence to be built up. In addition, their need for help and guidance through course content, tasks and assignments and information about the criteria being used to assess acceptable performance will all vary from person to person. Pratt (1988) has argued that the level of dependency of any learner is a temporary and situationally determined state, depending on the learner's competence, commitment and confidence.

- The first 'classic open' model, as represented here by the Maths GCSE workshop, can be seen to be assuming a medium to high level of dependency among its students. That is, it provides a medium to high level of support with a high level of directedness.
- The second model, the two-phase initial group model, represented here by the 'headstart training' and by the 'initial counter training' makes an assumption of an initial high dependency among trainees by providing high tutor direction and high support. However, the 'headstart' training continues to assume a high level of dependency through its continuing use of highly structured competency assessment materials and its mentors.
- A similar assumption of initial high dependency, but subsequent reducing learner dependency appears to underpin the 'progressive attenuation' model represented here by the 'initial counter training for agency staff (model 4).
- The assumptions underlying the 'club sandwich' model, represented here by model 3, the 'supervisors' course, are not so clear-cut. Different assumptions appear to be made at different points. Thus, in sending texts for independent study by the students, the assumption of low dependency is made, while the follow-up group work assumes high dependency.
- The final model 5, represented by the 'independent learning using a distance package' model, presents some difficulties in relation to identifying the underlying assumptions about learner dependency. The apparent freedom of the individual to choose their mode of study suggests a relatively low level of dependency is being assumed. This is supported by the fact that the provision

of media-based courses is not accompanied by any form of tutorial or mentor support, but comprises purely self-study packages which may be text, video or CD-ROM-based. However, the major alternative of intensive group-based tutor-led courses suggests an assumption of medium to high dependency.

Testing the models out against the assumptions they appear to make about the degree of learner dependency for which they are catering is revealing, but is by no means the whole story. It must be remembered that the models in use are each meeting different objectives. So, for example, with the exam-based courses provided by FE Colleges, such as the Maths GCSE course, the reported overriding concern is that the students should 'pass the exams and then move on either to further study or into employment' (McCollum, A and Calder, J). For national companies providing initial training, however, the concern is to ensure that all staff in specific jobs acquire basic competencies to the same comparable national standard. In the models examined in this section, we saw two rather different ways of achieving this aim. One assumed high dependency at all stages; the other started with high dependency but then had a formal 'attenuation' period in which the intensity and type of support was reduced.

The next chapter examines the effectiveness of student learning through open, flexible and distance methods. As previously mentioned, for many professionals, attitudes to such approaches are mixed. Certainly, perceptions about their effectiveness for different types of vocational education and training vary considerably, and do not always match the evidence which has been collected now over some time. The link between insights from professionals in the field and from learning theory is explored in order to understand the problems and potential of using these methods in vocational education and training.

Chapter 5

The effectiveness of open and flexible approaches

Introduction

The advantages of distance, open and flexible provision for education and training are well rehearsed. It is seen as a way of providing mass education at low cost; of minimizing travel costs and disruptions to work, and of introducing choice into the timing and duration of study and relevance into content of study. In other words, it is seen by many as being more effective than traditional forms of education in meeting the specific education and training needs of a wide range of people. The question for many educators and trainers, however, is whether the undoubted cost and access advantages of distance, open and flexible approaches to vocational education and training are outweighed by a reduction in the effectiveness of students' learning.

Why the issue of effectiveness is important

Just because open learning material is available, or because people participate in training, does not mean that it is necessarily effective for them. Stakeholders in vocational education and training at the craft and technician level will ask how open and flexible approaches compare with more traditional approaches to training. There can be considerable upfront costs associated with introducing open and flexible learning approaches into training settings. The question is, therefore, whether there is reliable evidence which shows how effective open, flexible and distance approaches are as training options. This chapter will focus on the effectiveness of both the process of training through open and flexible routes, and on the outcomes of the training.

What stakeholders mean by effectiveness

The evidence suggests that not only do the different stakeholders in vocational education and training (VETTOL) use different criteria when they assess effectiveness, but that there is considerable variation within stakeholder groups about what constitutes effective training, and that this has been the case for some time.

FE College tutors

The problems associated with attempting to identify learning effectiveness are well understood by tutors. In our study FE tutors made the point strongly that their aim was to maximize the chances of the students achieving their objectives. Learning effectiveness among FE tutors was seen in terms of:

- whether or not qualifications had been gained
- the extent to which students had gained or developed the characteristics, which were seen as necessary for successful future study and training.

In other words, whether the aims they had initially identified for the students had been achieved. Other sorts of indicator of learning effectiveness which some tutors mentioned they would look for in OFL courses included:

- the number of telephone calls resulting from problems
- the quality of the assignments submitted and
- student performance in oral examinations.

[Learning effectiveness]. Well who for? Is it effective for me? My employer? Whoever pays the fees? Is the outcome the college results? For me personally, [it is] effectiveness in practice. People may come in with preconceived ideas... I question and question the nature [of people's strong opinions] and see that they have moved...

[Learning effectiveness] comes from the very start, making sure that the right people get on to the right course. Not setting people up to fail or sending them in the wrong direction. You have to see that the modules are appropriate, that content is set and at an appropriate level for understanding but stretches them and covers exact objectives (FE College tutors).

Source: Calder *et al.* (1995)

Company trainers

Company trainers also showed a sophisticated appreciation of the problems inherent in trying to define and to measure the learning effectiveness of a specific mode of learning or approach to teaching. The sorts of example which were given included changes in work patterns, work process improvements and acquiring or improving competences in the use of new technology tools. In other words, quite specific changes might be expected from a course which focused on particular job skills.

The main focus of the training is to help people to do their current job and to integrate them into the department they are working in.

Training is provided so that people can do their jobs correctly and with confidence.

Training should provide clear guidelines to trainees along with the appropriate skills and knowledge and confidence to do the job (In-company trainers).

Source: Calder *et al.* (1995)

Differences in the purpose of the training did affect aims and, therefore, how effectiveness was perceived. Trainers engaged in induction training argued that if trainees could carry out the job for which they had been trained correctly and confidently then the training was effective. This view of the 'whole' job was in turn subsumed by the view that effective training meant that the newly trained person should fit into the department, and should be easily integrated into the workplace. In other words, they should not be seen as a separate and independent employee but as a member of a team, with the success of the team and the contribution of that person to the team being an important aim of the training. Thus, they saw the effectiveness of the training in terms of the improvement in:

- the individual's capability to do the job
- the individual's capacity to work as a member of a team
- the individual's capacity to 'fit into the department'.

Implicit here was the expectation of behaviour changes in the employee. It was recognized by the training manager concerned that the implication of this view was that 'team training' should have a much higher profile.

The criteria for the learning effectiveness of courses specifically related to the introduction of new machines or new procedures were very clear: the employees who had been trained should be able to implement and use the new machinery or the new procedures quickly in the workplace.

Tutors tend to see themselves as providing skills training. [The course] develops skills necessary to operate and maintain the machine. The courses are tightly geared to ensuring that everyone possible reaches at least the minimum level of competence on all key tasks (In-company technical and engineering tutors).

Source: Calder *et al.* (1995)

More problematic were the courses that taught management and supervisory skills. One tutor made the point that among the skills to be taught was the need, with some students, to first create in the student an awareness and understanding of the need for those skills.

Employers

In 1991, a study by BDO Binder Hamlyn concluded that 'companies tend to value training by cost and number of courses attended, rather than in terms of meeting business aims or targets' (Woodcock, 1991).

> We have a variety of training methods. They're very keen on cost effectiveness. That's the main motive (department manager, retail store).

In part, this may be because of the lack of any other easily collected and accessed data available to companies. In the same year, Temple (1991) reported on a British Steel study looking at learners' recall and retention of course material. In it she commented on the lack of objective data available on CBT courses in relation to conventional lecture type courses. Hawkridge *et al.* (1988), in discussing effectiveness of company training in relation to computer-based training, drew attention to the different criteria of employers and employees when he commented that 'companies want to exploit training techniques that either cost less for the same degree of effectiveness, or achieve greater effectiveness for the same cost', before going on to argue that 'what employees want is training, and retraining, that enables them to do the job well and safely. Only then can they gain greater job satisfaction. Of greatest value to the company is training that makes employees well-motivated and more competent'.

In the changing and competitive environment within which companies have to work, there is frequently the need to rapidly update large numbers of staff at decreasing cost. This means that the logistics of the timing of the training can have important knock-on effects on its effectiveness (Case Study 5.1).

Government

Job satisfaction and employee motivation appear to be less typical of employers' concerns than issues of cost and retention of knowledge. When we look at the criteria used by government, a rather mixed set of criteria appears to be in place. The criteria mentioned in the press release of the White Paper, 'Competitiveness: Helping Business to Win', in 1994 which introduced, among other things, modern apprenticeships, focused on simple performance indicators such as:

Case Study 5.1: Post Office Technical and Engineering Branch

The rapid growth in new technologies and the need to implement and utilize new machinery quickly in the workplace provided much of the impetus to the technical training providers adopting open learning methods. The question of the best point in time for the training to take place remains problematic. Some tutors feel that while ideally the trainees should first become familiar with the machines in their own workplace prior to training, the reality is that, due to the need to train large numbers when new machines are being introduced, staff may have to take the training course some months before the machine actually arrives at the workplace.

Open and flexible learning was used both to induct large numbers of staff dispersed thinly over large geographical areas, and to update large numbers of staff within very tight deadlines. There were problems with trying to get large numbers of staff through machinery updating courses in that the timing of the arrival of new machines and of the training courses did not always coincide.

Source: Calder *et al.* (1995)

- exam pass rates
- numbers going into higher education and
- proportion of young people training at work.

The statement and subsequent debate in Parliament, however, did mention rigorous standards, motivation of individuals, achievement of technical and supervisory skills and up-to-date skills.

Trainees

For trainees who are undertaking training as a condition of their job, there is no problem about what constitutes their main goal. The need to satisfactorily complete the course is taken for granted (Case Study 5.2).

The clarity of goals for trainees who are undertaking training for their future jobs can depend on their own drive and commitment, and the extent to which they see their future as being with a particular employer, or in a clearly defined type of role. The extracts from comments from trainees shown in (Example 5.1) are typical in their range. In particular, the need

- to understand what is being taught in relation to their work
- to prepare for further study
- to prepare for future job demands

are identified.

Case Study 5.2: 'Describe in your own words what you think your course is about...'

'My course was about the practical and technical background to process plant operation. How to apply the knowledge gained and understanding the principles behind the practice. *Its not what you know – its what you understand of what you know, thats what education is all about!*' [trainee's emphases]

'To assist in providing me with an underpinning knowledge in order to give me an understanding of the processes I deal with, and give me a first foot on the ladder to higher qualifications'.

'The course which I'm undertaking at the moment is preparing me for situations and equipment which I'm likely to come across and hopefully overcome in the future, if I was to be offered a job by my employer. The course hopefully goes to such an extent that if I was offered a job, then the knowledge gained from the course would enable me to extend my career to a higher level, and improve the effectiveness of the employers workforce'.

Trainees studying City and Guilds 0600 Part 11/BTEC National in Process Operations

---

Where there is no particular job yet in sight, there can be considerable difficulties for a trainee in that their needs may be for courses which will open up opportunities to them. There will be considerable risk to the individual if they focus down on too much in terms of trying to meet the needs of a particular employer.

It appears that each of the different groups of stakeholders represented in Example 5.1 sees the purposes of vocational education and training somewhat differently. The issue of concern about the government's views is the lack of any evidence of strategic level aims for vocational training. The focus appears to be primarily on performance indicators, with the implication that any increase must be seen as a positive achievement. To some extent, this may be because of the lack of evidence about the effectiveness of training. The simple overview picture provided by the reported focus on cost and number of courses attended is likely to be a result of the problems encountered by training managers in getting appropriate feedback on the effectiveness of the courses they provide. In practice, there appears to be little in the way of feedback to colleges, or to company trainers and training managers about the effectiveness of their training.

'...there's no follow-up whatsoever...going to talk to managers they wouldn't know what you were talking about. They wouldn't have any concept of any improvement' (In-company trainer).

Example 5.1: Summary chart of views on learning effectiveness criteria

The Government ....
- exam pass rates
- numbers going into higher education and proportion of young people training at work
- rigorous standards
- motivation of individuals
- achievement of up-to-date technical and supervisory skills

Companies...............................
- cost and number of courses attended meeting business aims or targets

Trainers.....................................
- whether people helped to do their current job
- integration of trainees into their department

Tutors ....
- whether qualifications gained
- development of study skills
- whether the initial aims identified for the students had been achieved

Trainees ....
- to understand what is being taught in relation to their work
- to prepare for further study
- to prepare for future job demands

How do we measure learning effectiveness?

Before you can measure something, you have to be quite clear about precisely what it is you are measuring. Rumble sees effectiveness as being concerned with outputs (Rumble, 1997) – outputs which are relevant to the needs of the clients. He also draws attention to the need for criteria against which success can be measured.

The problematic nature of trying to establish the learning effectiveness of distance, open and flexible provision is well illustrated in our own project. Learning effectiveness is not just a matter of the interaction of the learner with learning or training provision. Context must be taken into account, and in the vocational training world, contexts can change rapidly. We already understand to some extent the importance of the effect of multiple stakeholders in assessing the success of provision for adults (Calder, 1993). The question which research into learning effectiveness in the vocational field needs to move on to address is what contextual variables are the key ones? In order to do this, however, it is necessary first to make explicit the extent to which the term 'learning effectiveness' enjoys a common understanding, or whether the term embraces a variety of understandings.

Problems in measuring effectiveness

One of the main problems in trying to determine the effectiveness of anything is that you need to be clear not only about what the goals are, but also what relative weightings you would attach to each of those goals. For example, it has been remarked that the perfect open learning course should satisfy three conditions: it should be of high quality, be low cost and be quick to produce. Unfortunately, in reality, only two of these three criteria can ever be met at the same time.

> The main criterion [of learning effectiveness] was how effective the person was back in the workplace. Clerical or technical topics were seen as relatively easy to measure in that staff should be able to do something after training which they hadn't been able to before training. However with management related topics, the problem of trying to assess whether a person 'managed' better after the course than they did before the course was seen as presenting considerable difficulties. In particular, the subjective nature of any such evaluation was commented on.
>
> Because of their distancing from the training role, line managers would find it difficult to identify improvements in performance, but would tend to notice if the training wasn't working.
>
> *Source*: Calder *et al.* (1995)

If we take the issue of high-quality training, again, criteria of what constitutes high quality will vary depending on whom you speak with – does it include the development of self-confidence in the learner, study skills competence, enthusiasm for further self-development, for the acquisition of a higher level of skill or a willingness to follow instructions without questioning them?

The problem is compounded in relation to the effectiveness of open, flexible and distance methods in vocational education and training because of the number of stakeholders involved. The goals they hold for a particular programme or training course may not only be different but possibly contradictory. Even within the same company, the department manager may want staff trained to meet the demands of their job as it currently stands; the senior management of the company may want the training to prepare staff for the medium or longer term in order to contribute to the improvement of department and of the company (Bailey, 1993), and the trainee may simply want a qualification which is portable – which is recognized outside the company.

The difficulty for the larger stakeholders is admirably summed up by Burnes (1996) in a discussion on the managment of change. He suggests that '*Training, as a mechanism for change, is unlikely to succeed on its own* [author's italics]. This is because it concentrates on the individual and not the organizational level'. He goes on to quote Burke as arguing that 'although training may lead to individual change and in some cases to small group change, there is scant evidence that attempting to change the individual will in turn change the organization'. This question is also taken up by Farnes *et al.*, (1994) in relation to the contribution of management education through open learning to individual, organizational and societal change in the context of the transition of Central and Eastern Europe to a market economy. They concluded that:

> For an organization to maximize the adoption and application of what is learnt from the courses employers should – sponsor more than one student, sponsor those from senior levels, ensure that they are in frequent contact with each other and enable them to work together to make changes: encourage the transfer of what is learnt to other employees through normal work channels, meetings and special events such as training sessions.

Measures currently used

The fact that a range of different characteristics were identified as important in considering the learning effectiveness of a course does not mean that there were measures available by which the effectiveness could be measured. A number of the criteria identified in Example 5.1 would present a clear challenge for those attempting to construct appropriate performance indicators. The measures which are used vary from the direct to a variety of indirect objective and subjective measures. While the FE courses were most likely to have direct measures in the form of assessment data, some in-company courses also used this approach. Most notable were the competency-based courses, such as the headstart programme operated by Safeway, in which personal records were kept of the acquisition of each competency, as well as the Post Office technical training programmes in which key competencies were again carefully assessed during the residential component of the course. Indirect methods included 'objective' measures such as productivity changes, as well as 'subjective' measures such as line managers' assessments of changes in work practice.

The difference in approach to measuring learning effectiveness between different types of course was remarked upon by one trainer. Testing people on technical courses was seen as relatively straightforward, but for management and supervisory skills, the aim was competency in the workplace, and so the trainer was seen as having no role in the assessment of those skills.

Using feedback sheets

Current methods used extensively within the in-company training courses were the 'end-of-course' feedback sheets. These were assessments by the participants of the usefulness and effectiveness of the course in terms of its applicability to their job. The response rate to these, however, does appear to vary considerably, as do the formal procedures for monitoring and incorporating the results of the feedback. There did not appear to be any equivalent feedback within the FE courses involved in our study. Feedback sheets, often called 'happy sheets' by the trainers who use them, usually consist of a single sheet with simple questions listed on it. They are designed to be completed very quickly by trainees – usually at the end of a short face-to face course or section of course. They are usually anonymous, and are returned to the trainer before the course finally closes. Their advantage is that they do provide a record of trainee responses to identifed aspects of the course. This can be used by trainers to modify those parts of the course which seem to present trainees with most difficulties. They can also be used as hard 'evidence' of the success or usefulness of particular courses. Their disadvantage is that they may only be filled in by a minority of trainees, depending on the emphasis given to them by the trainer; the comments of the trainees may be muted by the knowledge that the trainer will read them; and they deal only with the immediate reactions of the trainees rather than a considered response after the trainee has attempted to implement what has been learned when back in the workplace.

If they liked the subject and they liked you then you tend to get favourable feedback. If they didn't like the subject then the chances are that you could get unfavourable feedback but no one is actually going along in say three months time and looking at the improvement and effectiveness of the work (In-company trainer).

Constant monitoring

Where training is supervised by workplace-based mentors, or by line managers it does allow for regular monitoring. This includes not only the progress of the trainee, but also monitoring of the training process itself (Case Study 5.3).

Case Study 5.3: Safeway

There was a strong consensus amongst Safeway's staff that the new training approach used for initial training for retail staff and Management Training Programme combining the use of workbooks, hands on experience and close supervision provided practical, relevant and effective training programmes.

Perceived Learning Outcomes and criteria for success: The key outcome of training was viewed as being that trainees could carry out the job correctly and confidently, and this was therefore ultimately viewed as the key measure of success; Training should provide clear guidelines to trainees along with the appropriate skills and knowledge and the confidence to do the job. To judge whether such outcomes were met managers used a formal structured system of review and assessment, and also used an ongoing and informal method of simply taking the time to talk to trainees;

'I talk directly with them and ask them questions about what they're doing and why, I spend time with people and set objectives and discuss how to follow through and review those objectives on a regular basis'.

The assumption of success: Training in Safeways usually takes place when people have either been newly appointed or promoted to a new position, thus they have already passed the test as it were and it is expected that they will 'succeed' in their training; as one store manager observed:

'The management training is 6–8 months, if they need more time its okay, because of the structured interviews. We think we have the right people so we will give more time if they need it, it's worth the investment. It could be 6, 7 or 8 months if they're slow they have to get the basics right at the start or the foundations are not strong enough, it is a big investment of time so they have to be careful choosing mentors, if a store manager is a bad mentor it would reflect badly on him'.

Training is provided so that people can do their jobs correctly and with confidence. Learning effectiveness is therefore directly related to work performance and training is very closely tied to the workplace. While on the job training has many advantages in terms of relevance, practicality and convenience it does however create some problems, both for the trainers and the trainees, as outlined below.

On the job training: The main focus of training is to help people to do their current job and to integrate them into the department they are working in, the training is therefore literally as and when they do the job. Here a staff training manager describes the main problem associated with such on the job training.

'We take people on and expect them to do on the job training and do the job before they're trained properly to do it… that's not the right way to do it'…

Whilst department managers and store managers have a central role to play in overseeing and assessing training, they themselves have little training in how to fulfil that role. The training programme is highly structured in that assessment is closely and clearly tied to competencies within the job profile, and there are clear procedures for review and assessment, for example they have to sign off competency areas as they acquire them… However the value of the training can vary considerably according to the managers' input as they may be 'guessing grades and training needs'.

Source: Calder *et al.* (1995)

The advantages identified by staff using this approach are that the training is closely tied to the workplace and to workplace needs. Similarly, its effectiveness is directly monitored within the workplace by senior staff. The disadvantages are that the training and monitoring functions do need to be recognized as part of the manager's job. Training does need to be given in how to exercise these additional responsibilities. There are an increasing number of instances where companies and local colleges collaborate, with the college providing a formal monitoring and assessment service for the company, and where the need for supervision and assessment of competency-based skills is intermittent. However, where there is a regular and sustained need for assessment, pressure is on the company to find its own solution (Case Study 5.4).

Case Study 5.4: Examples of assessment strategies from three companies offering NVQs using open and flexible methods

In Severn Trent Water, supervisory staff were not accredited assessors but had received training in assessment. They were responsible for monitoring craft level staff and determining when they were ready for formal assessment for their NVQ level 2 in Water Industry Standards. In Tesco and Price Waterhouse, the companies' own staff registered for formal certification as assessors after successfully undertaking training for and completing the Training and Development Lead Body (TDLB) units in assessment, D32 and D33. The opportunity to become an accredited NVQ assessor was seen as a good training and development opportunity for individual supervisors and managers; giving them the opportunity to take part in assessment, learn the value of having a set of clear standards and developing assessors' analytic skills.

Source: Calder and Newton (1995)

However, not all companies are moving in the direction of involving managers closely in the training process (Case Study 5.5).

College tutors also tend to use constant monitoring of the progress of their students. Again, the procedures which are followed do vary considerably. Some students on open, flexible and distance courses have their own tutors who keep an extremely close eye on their progress and who may liaise with the students' sponsors if progress is considered to be unsatisfactory. Other courses, particularly those which use a workshop approach, may see the responsibility for progress as being with the student. In such cases, it may be that assessment or exam results are the main form of feedback used.

Special studies

One response of those training managers who are particularly concerned about the lack of information on the effectiveness of training within companies is to institute their own follow-up studies. This can involve setting up training files on employees, and sending out short questionnaires to their managers following any participation in training. Unfortunately, in the examples we came across, the response rate from line managers was too low to draw any conclusions.

Case Study 5.5:   Inland Revenue

Some tutors felt that over the last few years the involvement of line managers in training had been steadily decreasing to the extent that the training centre was now being approached to provide the type of training which originally would have been provided by line managers.

'Yes, they would detect that there was a shortfall in this person's knowledge; and this comes back to the original problem... that a problem is seen as a problem now for us to solve rather than a problem for them to solve as a line manager'.

Because of their 'distancing' from the training role, line managers would find it difficult to identify improvements in performance, but would tend to notice if the training wasn't working. At the same time, the point was made that to a considerable extent, the closeness of the line manager to the member of staff in training would affect their ability to comment on the effectiveness of training being received.

Source: Calder and Newton (1995)

It depends who's actually done the training. If the Revenue Executives are being trained, their line managers are [Tax] Inspectors... With those the chances are you probably wouldn't get any opinion on whether they'd become more effective. Now with Revenue Officers their line manager is the Revenue Executive and if you were to interview the Revenue Executive, because they're in daily contact and they should see a lot of the Revenue Officers work, you might actually be able to detect whether the Revenue Executive considers there's been effectiveness (Inland Revenue trainer).

Other methods used included surveys of line managers and surveys of staff in relation to their general satisfaction with training provision. A noticeable feature about the methods reported for trying to measure learning effectiveness within the courses selected from the in-company training was the growth in the recognition of the need to get such data. A common feature, however, were the problems experienced in the attempts which had been made to collect this type of data. In particular, attempts to involve line managers appeared to be particularly problematic in terms of actually getting responses from them.

Achieving effective learning

The question for those involved with or considering the use of open, flexible or distance methods for vocational training is whether the fact that open and flexible approaches are used has any effect on students' learning. We have seen that some tutors and trainers who use open and flexible learning methods feel that this approach is more suitable for some types of students than for others. Learning theory suggests that the factors which are likely to play a role in the effectiveness of learning are more likely to lie with other factors.

Learning theory

So, when is effective learning likely to occur? One view (Ford, 1981) is that effective learning is most likely to occur when students:

- have sufficient underpinning knowledge to support learning involving higher levels of abstraction
- are aware that they can approach learning in different ways, and have the study skills to be able to choose the most appropriate approach for the learning task specified
- have goals for learning which match those for the course.

Two of the authorities on whose work Ford drew were:

- the Gothenburg group
- Gordon Pask.

The research of the Gothenburg group has linked different levels of understanding by students with the approach to learning they adopt (Case Study 5.6). Their research into the ways in which students read a selected passage showed there are basically two different approaches in the way in which people undertake the task of learning:

- a *surface* approach
- a *deep* approach.

Case Study 5.6: Gothenburg group

Learners taking a surface approach usually focus on the different pieces of information, often memorizing by rote learning. The emphasis is on being able to anticipate the question which they might be asked, and to *reproduce* the pieces of information which they have memorized. Such students tend to be conscious of the conditions in which they are tested and to be anxious about them.

In contrast, learners taking a deep approach usually look for the linkages and connections between pieces of information in order to understand the sense of what is being taught. The emphasis is on the learner being able to *interpret* what they have learned in relation to their own knowledge and past experience.

In the mid-1970s, at the same time as the studies were being carried out in Gothenburg, Gordon Pask in London was also carrying out a series of studies to try to discover the strategies students used in their learning.

So what sort of thinking process does a person go through when they are learning something? Is it the same for everyone? Is it the same in all situations, or for different sorts of learning tasks? Experience, common sense and research are all in general agreement here – that people do differ from each other in the way they respond to learning opportunities, and they differ in the way they respond to similar learning opportunities on different occasions and for different purposes. The thinking processes or the cognitive style which a learner uses are generally identified as one of two possibilities. Many labels are used to describe these two alternatives, but one set, as identified by Gordon Pask, is termed 'holist versus serialist' (Case Study 5.7).

Case Study 5.7: Gordon Pask

Pask argued that distinctive learning strategies do exist. He used the term *style* to describe a disposition to adopt one form or type of learning strategy. From a series of experiments carried out during the seventies, he concluded that most people could acquire the general skill of 'learning to learn'. That is people are able to approach new situations or new topics and make their own way. They are able to 'organize and assimilate a body of subject matter with minimal direction from outside'. His experiments using both holist and serialist learners in different learning tasks convinced him that personal consistency in learning style outweighed the demands of context. Also that a mismatch of learning style with teaching style led to no relevant learning.

Learners who use a holist approach tend to look for similarities in sets of data or information rather than differences. So, for example, they use analogies or generalizations. One type of holist learner needs and uses examples given within the material to be learned. The other type create their own. Discovery learning is one example of how this is applied.

Serialist learners are of two types. The one who progresses logically step-by-step, assimilating each stage in turn, looking for guidance as to the next topic to be tackled. The other is the rote learner, following the prescribed path, relying upon memory rather than on understanding and comprehension, but often doing well in exams.

Source: Pask (1988)

Laurillard (1984) describes the difference between the two sets of research as follows:

> [The Gottenburg studies deal with] the learning process from the students' point of view. The power of this type of research is that it allows us to investigate a process that is essentially internal by obtaining students' descrip-

tions of the experiences of learning... They make the students' perceptions of the structure of the material the focus of their investigation. Pask, like the information processing theorists, takes the structure of the material as given, and investigates what students do with that information, or how they process it.

Noel Entwistle, at Lancaster University, continued the work of the Gothenburg group (so called because the main researchers, Ference Marton and Roger Säljö were based in Sweden at the University of Gothenburg) by developing a questionnaire or inventory which enabled the student's approach to learning to be identifed. The technique he used was to look for the underlying factors which distinguished between different forms of student motivation and study strategies. As he explains in his book *Styles of Learning and Teaching* (Entwistle, 1981), the Lancaster inventory drew on the Gothenburg work and on Pask's ideas.

Learning theory then clearly suggested that students' approach to learning was, in effect, a personal characteristic. It could be affected by the context in which the learning took place as well as by the task which was set. For example, Laurillard concluded that the type of exercise or problem set by the teacher could influence the student's choice of learning style. This was illustrated through the example of reading tasks compared with problem-solving tasks. The importance of the assessment strategy in encouraging learners to adopt a particular style of learning became widely accepted in higher education.

Case Study 5.8: Andragogy

Andragogy was the term used by Malcolm Knowles in 1980 to describe his theory of teaching adults. Its articulation and promotion by Knowles stimulated debate and thinking about the similarities and differences between the ways in which adults and children learned. At the heart of the concept is the view that adults see themselves as self-directing, but that they often do not apply this view of themselves to education and training situations. The four fundamental ideas which comprise andragogy were spelled out by Knowles as follows:

1. Adults become more self-directed as they get older, although it does depend on the situation they face.

2. Adults can draw upon their experiences as part of the learning process. Thus discussion groups, problem-solving and other experiential techniques help them to learn more effectively.

3. Adults recognize that they have learning needs because the problems they have to cope with in life will often involve them in having to learn something new. Therefore, adult education programmes should be related to real life tasks and problems.

4. Adults want to apply what they have just learned.

During this same period, the work of adult educators in the US and in Canada did much to open up the issue of adult learning with considerable strides being made in our thinking about how adults actually learn. The idea of the adult learner as an 'empty vessel' waiting to be filled had been the predominant one for many teachers and trainers. It now became clear that people continued to learn and to grow throughout life, learning through both formal instruction and through self-directed learning activity (Case Study 5.8).

Students' approaches to learning

A substantial body of literature has been established, which shows that there is a relationship between the learning process and different types of learning outcome. The learning process here refers to the qualitative differences in the ways in which learners approach their learning. However, the research on which the majority of this work is based comes almost exclusively from the field of higher education. The question is whether such concepts as 'deep' and 'surface' learning have any validity when applied to participants in basic vocational education and training. The 'deep' approach to learning is concerned with understanding the material being learned; with relating new ideas to existing knowledge and with synthesizing the new and the old ideas. In contrast, the 'surface' approach to learning is concerned with acquiring knowledge or skills without relating it to an existing base of knowledge. Thus, rote learning and memorizing are typical of the learning methods which might be used with a 'surface' approach to learning.

In order to examine the relevance of learning approaches with this population, and to identify how students undertaking vocational education and training approach their studies, we asked the trainees in our study to complete the Entwistle and Tait inventory of learning styles. This inventory has had extensive testing including its use with students undertaking open and flexible learning (OFL) study. The particular version used was the 44-item inventory with an additional 15 items added for the purposes of this project.

From the factor analyses undertaken, the most important five factors, which emerged from the initial analysis in terms of participants' approaches to learning were:

- strategic approach
- surface approach
- deep approach
- lack of direction
- self-confidence.

These underlying factors would all play important roles in determining how trainees approached their training, and hence in the effectiveness of that training. For example, students who adopted a strategic approach were concerned about conditions for study, made efforts to get the most important details right, had clear aims and were highly motivated.

Students who adopted a surface approach tended to feel at sea with the amount of material they had to cope with, worried about their work, couldn't make sense of things, couldn't see any overall picture and generally felt they couldn't cope. In contrast, students with a deep approach need to think things out for themselves, try to work out what is really wanted in a piece of work, think through ideas, see how ideas fit together, to see the reasoning and try to reach own conclusions.

There were also students with a clear motivational problem, who suffered from a lack of direction in their studies. They didn't know why they had decided to do the course, felt it was not their own choice and that they had drifted into the course, perhaps because they wanted to please others.

Finally, the degree of self-confidence which students felt about their studies emerged as an important fact: in terms of whether they felt they had a good grasp of subject, found the set work easy, were able to grasp things for themselves, and whether they experienced difficulties in making sense of new information or ideas.

The further analysis using these factors revealed that while there was no significant difference between students undertaking OFL study and those on traditional courses, there was a significant difference between participants on the courses within the FE sector compared with those in the in-company sector on two of the factors. The first was on the proportion of students and trainees who tended to adopt a surface approach with a significantly higher proportion of those undertaking college courses than those on in-company courses being likely to have a surface approach (see Table 5.1). Similarly, in-company trainees exhibited a significantly higher degree of self-confidence about their studies than did students on FE College courses (see Table 5.2).

Table 5.1 *Surface learning approach by mode and sector of course*

| | Traditional | | OFL | |
| | FE | In-company | FE | In-company |
Surface approach	%	%	%	%
low	24	53	29	55
medium	37	36	32	22
high	39	11	38	22

n = 440

(Cramer's V = 0.2 significant @ .00001 level)

The final analysis run then produced two major factors from the 59 items. These were:

- deep and strategic
- surface.

Table 5.2 *Self-confidence score by mode and sector of course*

| | Traditional | | OFL | |
| | FE | In-company | FE | In-company |
Self-confident approach	%	%	%	%
low	36	12	34	10
medium	42	45	44	54
high	22	43	29	36

n = 440

(Cramer's V = 0.2 significant @ .0001 level)

A deep and strategic approach here is taken to mean participants who not only like to think things through for themselves but also like to get things organized so that their conditions for study are right, that they know what the key information is, that they go about their studies in a systematic way and who are generally determined to succeed. These two underlying factors – surface and deep and strategic – explained 53 per cent of the variance of the items. Although, as previously mentioned, there was a significant difference between course participants in different sectors in terms of those holding a surface approach, the chi square for those holding a deep and strategic approach showed no such difference (see Table 5.3).

Table 5.3 *Learning approach by mode of course studied*

| | Traditional | | OFL | |
| | FE | In-company | FE | In-company |
Deep/strategic approach:	%	%	%	%
low	32	28	39	28
medium	38	44	25	39
high	30	28	35	33

n = 440

(Chi square and Cramer's V not significant)

That the factors which emerged from the factor analysis bore such a close match to those which have emerged from research in higher education is extremely important. An exploratory approach was deliberately adopted so that all possible emergent factors could be considered and reviewed. It should be noted that the factor 'deep and strategic' has been previously noted in the literature (Richardson, 1994), although other work with a different student body identifies 'deep' separately from 'strategic'.

It is now clear from the work done so far that learning approaches adopted by people undertaking basic vocational education and training, through both the FE sector and in-company training, can be established through the use of a self-completion inventory and that the approaches identified are very similar, albeit not totally identical to those established for students on other kinds and levels of courses.

What is not clear at this point is why there should be the differences there are between FE course participants and those on in-company training courses. It could be speculated that trainees who are already in work feel much less under stress during training than do unemployed people who form a large proportion of those on FE College courses. Similarly, the summative assessment for qualification purposes may have a much higher profile for students on public courses than on in-company courses. Whatever the reason, this is clearly an area that needs further investigation. At the moment it is not at all clear whether the higher likelihood of a surface approach to learning in FE Colleges is an attribute which students bring with them and which tutors, therefore, need to address, or whether it is caused by the teaching approaches adopted in FE Colleges. It must be said that this alternative looks rather unlikely given the range of modes and variety of teaching approaches adopted in the courses which we investigated. The intriguing aspect is the lack of a significant difference between those following traditional courses and those following open and flexible courses in the way in which they approach their studies.

Learning effectiveness then is a more elusive concept than we might have expected initially. In spite of this, different stakeholders still need to make their own judgements about the likely effectiveness of training programmes with which they may be involved. The next chapter examines in more detail the questions which one group of stakeholders in particular – training providers – have to address when selecting a training programme which uses an open or flexible approach. A common set of critical factors which are linked to the successful implementation of open, flexible and distance approaches to vocational education and training are identifed.

Chapter 6

Selecting and implementing appropriate solutions

Introduction

The key question for companies is how they can most effectively and efficiently manage training within their organizations. However, given the need to respond to a variety of individual learning needs and the wide-ranging methods by which training can be provided, this is a complex question, which is not helped by the distinct lack of 'simple operational guidelines indicating what actually should be done in the organization on Monday morning' (Sloman, 1994).

Sloman argues that organizations now have increasingly complex training requirements. Therefore, in order to deliver effective training, the modern organization needs to adopt a radically new approach to training. Thus, one of the key challenges facing the training provider lies in the diversity of training provision both in terms of training needs and in terms of training options.

Earlier chapters identified the myriad range of factors and considerations which may underlie the decision to use open learning for vocational training purposes. This chapter reviews some of the factors which need to be considered in the selection and development of appropriate training programmes. It then goes on to explore some of the central practical challenges which those responsibile for the selection and provision of training need to face, from the need to clarify training roles and responsibilities, through to the implementation and evaluation of training courses. This chapter draws on a range of case study examples of open learning in action, and identifies a common set of critical factors which are linked to the successful implementation of open learning.

Key factors determining the selection of training programmes

In selecting appropriate training programmes, the training provider needs to address a number of issues which fall into four main areas of concern:

1. overall purpose of training
2. population targeted by the training programme
3. educational goals
4. needs of the organization.

The first section briefly reviews the main factors which we have identified as needing to be considered in the selection and development of appropriate training programmes.

The overall purpose of training

In terms of company training, the overall purpose of training is normally that trainees can do their job effectively. Thus, while specific training needs may vary widely from learning new technical skills to basic induction into company policy or procedures, the overall purpose which all training programmes will have in common is that the training provides relevant work skills which can be used effectively on the job. This concern has been a major driving force in company moves towards workplace learning whereby the learning process is integral to working processes and the workplace, and training is provided internally. As one company training provider observed:

> it is cost-effective and efficient to have training within the line and not divorced from local responsibilities. This is because training can be concentrated on skills that are entirely relevant to the job, while generic courses will inevitably cover some irrelevant territory (Saggers, 1994).

Littlefield (1994) argues that the advantage of tailored programmes as compared to generic training is that they can be more targeted, bring you faster change and can be very results-oriented. A key criticism of generic training, in addition to the fact that it covers areas which are not directly job-related is that there is a danger that the training is not necessarily transferred to the workplace, a concern apparently supported by Forrester's findings in a survey of retail training in which two-thirds of workers stated that their training had little or no effect on their job performance (Forrester *et al.*, 1995).

The emphasis on local responsibility for training, targeted training and application of skills in the workplace implies a shift in the responsibilities of line managers from a relatively passive role to a more active role, and also implies the need for closer working relationships between training providers, tutors and line managers so that there is the capacity for a flexible response to training needs and for personalizing provision to meet local needs.

The population targeted in the training programme

Employing organizations operate in different sectors, with different criteria for success, different management structures, also they are coping with different types of problems, and with very different sizes of workforce and staffing profiles. Using a framework developed by Joan Woodward and extended by Charles Perrow, it is possible to identify three key dimensions in analysing training needs.

---

1. one-off or small volume

2. large batch or mass volume

3. continuous flow or process volume

Source: adapted from discussion in Burnes (1996)

This list categorizes training needs by their size and flow. The training need of any organization, whatever its size, will fit one of these three groups. At the same time, the predictability of the need, and the extent to which routine or non-routine solutions may be used, will also play a key role in identifying an appropriate training solution.

One-off or small volume

Every trainer knows the problem of trying to get together at the same time enough students or trainees to form a reasonable group for training purposes. In theory, this problem should not matter with distance education, or with the one-to-one training offered by computer-based provision for example. While we found a number of positive examples using this approach in our study, such as IT training in FE Colleges, and updating on stock control and management using CD-ROMs for in-company training of sales assistants, it was equally clear that some trainees had experienced the worst form of unsupported distance learning, being simply directed to the local Resource Centre, which might be anything from a cupboard with a few manuals locked away, to a well-stocked room but with nobody available to advise, guide or support the learner in getting to grips with an unfamiliar form of learning.

Large batch or mass volume

Where demand can be forecast, the advantage of a standardized course available to large numbers appears to point quite unequivocally to some form of supported open learning. Situations such as the one at Severn Trent Water, which involve the once-off training of a large number of existing staff, followed by small-volume provision for new staff, were handled through the use of supported open learning involving a partnership between the company training department and the local college.

Continuous flow or process volume

For training managers, the ideal situation is one where there is a reliable and continuous flow of workers needing to be trained in a particular set of skills. Staff can be recruited, feedback organized, premises arranged in the sure knowledge that there will be no last minute changes. Unfortunately, we did not come across any examples in practice which fitted this scenario. In FE Colleges, competition between providers for students means that forward planning in terms of issuing contracts to staff and arranging premises can mean taking substantial financial risks. In-company training has to respond to the ebb and flow of numbers recruited and the variations in needs identified during staff development and staff appraisal interviews.

The educational goals

In terms of educational goals, concerns fall broadly into three categories. Firstly, there are specific skills which are required of the workforce. Thus, the educational goals would revolve around the workforce acquiring specific skills and knowledge such as the use of new technology, or knowledge of specific products or processes. Secondly, there is a broader set of concerns regarding the need for workers to fit in to the department or the company, requiring personal skills such as reliability and timekeeping, and interpersonal skills such as team work and cooperation. Lastly, there is concern regarding the quality of the learning skills possessed by the workforce; the educational goals being that workers learn how to learn more effectively and efficiently, that they learn how to be more flexible and adaptable, and that they become self-directed learners.

Furthermore, in looking at the effectiveness of different types of education and training provision in relation to achieving the educational goals, the problem is compounded because of the number of stakeholders involved and because of the range and often contradictory nature of the goals which they hold for a particular course or training programme. The department manager may want a member of staff who can meet all the demands of their job as it currently stands; the senior management of the company may want someone who can also contribute to the improvement of the department, whose future potential is being developed (Bailey, 1993); the individual who is undertaking the training may want a qualification which is recognized outside the company.

Our research shows that in order to take a 'human capital' approach, companies need to have a dual concern both to train the individual to achieve the course objectives and also to set this training in the context of their personal development. Rank Xerox, for example, has two routes for the identification of training needs, one is through the identification of individual or personal development needs and the other is through the identification of business need, that is, new knowledge or skills required in order to move the business forward. After departmental appraisals have been carried out, training needs are identified and action plans are drawn up for individuals. Similarly, Safeway has recently established a training scheme called

'Management Succession Planning' which was designed to appraise and assess the training needs of department managers and supervisors. Thus, in addition to a set training programme, there is a range of optional courses which can be selected according to individual needs.

The needs of the organization

As previously mentioned there are a whole range of different reasons why a provider may decide to introduce the use of distance, open or flexible learning. Ideally, with any learning need, the type of delivery chosen would be the one which is most appropriate to the circumstances of the learning. However, contextual factors can play an equal or even dominant role.

Within the wider context, the growth in the market approach to training has led to the situation where training provision is increasingly having to compete with other providers in the short term. Any developments which need a longer-term introduction, therefore, need careful handling. This is a particular problem when it comes to trying to get feedback from the 'clients' for example. Companies included in our research appreciated the need for some form of systematic feedback and evaluation of their courses, and training managers were trying different methods to introduce feedback from line managers and those who made the training needs' decisions. However, there are resource costs as well as time costs, and there is still a considerable gap between theory and practice in this area.

The needs of the organization or organizational context is also important in determining appropriate training options. A number of organizational conditions operate as constraints, which effectively delineate the format which the training programme will assume. Take the issue of training time. The company may aim for minimum disruption to the job, thus students may be expected to train in their own time. Or there may be pressure for the training to be undertaken in a short time scale, especially if the company encounters rapid change to which it must quickly adapt. The policy-making and decision-making structure within which training operates will also have a considerable effect on the type of new developments which can be planned and the speed with which they can be introduced. Within many FE Colleges, for instance, the departments operate very much as individual units. Thus, while innovation could quickly flower, there was often little learning across departments.

The training challenge

The challenges facing training providers is captured in the beguilingly simple statement that they must 'provide the right employees with the right skills at the right time' (Symons, 1994). However, as already mentioned, there is a high degree of complexity and variability involved in the decision-making process in relation to the development and implementation of training programmes. Work-related training and education encompasses diverse student populations, courses and learning environments. Therefore, variations in the effectiveness and suitability of different training programmes may be related to student differences, contextual differences and variations in the demands of different topic areas.

The possible patterns of interaction between the key variables identified are endless, and the contextual variables may often be at odds with the central aims of the training. For example, while a primary training objective is often that it should be directly job-related, factors relating to the target population or the organizational context may serve to undermine the organization's capacity to deliver job-related training and, therefore, serve to undermine the quality of the learning experience.

In our research four critical issues emerged in relation to the effective selection and implementation of open learning programmes:

1. There is a need for clarity regarding the training roles and responsibilities of line managers, tutors and training providers.
2. The production of good quality, appropriate learning materials and packages is dependent upon good communication between line managers, tutors and training providers to ensure the organizational effectiveness of training, ie to ensure that the identified training needs are met.
3. The use of open learning methods in relation to some skills and subject areas such as machine skills or mathematics was a matter of concern for a number of tutors who identified specific strategies for compensating for the potential weaknesses in open learning methods in relation to some courses.
4. Open learning methods will be more effective with some students and trainees than with others. There is, therefore, a need to make study support available to those who need it.

In order to understand more fully the challenges facing training providers, each of the four issues will be looked at in turn. A number of company responses will be explored, some of which you will already be familiar with, where their approach to achieving their aims in terms of overall purpose and education goals was largely determined by the organizational context and the nature of the target population. The central question is not whether different media are effective, but 'under what conditions one medium may be superior and which medium in which situation can bring about most learning' (Bates, 1981). Furthermore, the key to success is not only to identify the most appropriate method of provision but also to identify the strengths and weaknesses of the particular methods which are selected, for the critical ingredients for training success will vary according to the methods selected.

Shifting roles and responsibilities

The role of the line manager in relation to choosing appropriate training appears to be increasing with the growth in the market approach to training provision. Line managers are increasingly seen as having a key role to play in training needs assessment and with mentoring during training periods. For example, in the companies included in our research, entry on to training courses is often determined by the local office on the basis of the line managers' decisions and the development of personnel is seen as a direct responsibility of line managers.

The extent to which line managers adapt to their expanded training responsibilities varies widely and was identified as a critical problem by training staff, particularly in terms of the need for line managers to actively support trainees in the application of newly acquired skills and knowledge, to ensure that trainees had sufficient time to study, and to provide feedback to training managers about the quality of training provided. Training managers do try to give advice and guidance to managers about training options for staff, but feedback is not always forthcoming; nor does monitoring by senior staff of the exercise of that responsibility by the line manager necessarily take place.

There is, therefore, an urgent need to consider how line manager training responsibilities can become an integral part of their work so that their accountability for identifying training needs and selecting and implementing training programmes is clear and explicit. At Rank Xerox, for example, the idea has been put forward of incorporating the results of training into employee records as a stimulus to line managers to participate more fully in formally assessing the outcomes of training as well as the needs. In terms of ensuring that line managers take on board their training responsibilities, Safeway had developed the most comprehensive and clearly structured systems we had seen. For example, while management trainees are in the store it is the store manager's role to monitor trainees progress, ensuring that they receive the feedback and guidance which is so critical for their development. The store manager should ensure that trainees are formally given time on a weekly basis to establish training plans and agree weekly objectives, based on the operational competencies they need to achieve.

At the other end of the spectrum, we found examples where line managers were in practice becoming distanced from the training role. At Inland Revenue, for example, responsibility for achieving successful training outcomes appears to lie increasingly with the providers of training. Problems appear to occur because the extent to which the required outcomes are then practised in the workplace cannot be established and the locus of responsibility for training and for successful outcomes is not clear.

The production of course materials

The need to integrate training programmes with business objectives, and to provide appropriate knowledge and authentic work-based activities within training programmes, implies the need for course design and development to also be closely tied to the workplace through the close collaboration of training providers and those with responsibility for the delivery and implementation of training, ie course tutors and line managers.

Case Study 6.1: Inland Revenue

At the Inland Revenue open learning materials are produced in two separate centres and training can be delivered either in one of five regional centres, through residential courses or in the workplace. The Lincoln training centre has a small distance learning unit which is seen as being closely connected to the delivery side of the management programmes in that a number of staff work on both the distance teaching texts and the tutor-led components of the course. The role of the tutor is seen to be changing rapidly, as tutors have become closely involved in materials' production, which is seen as highly valuable in terms of having the materials validated by the trainees in that tutors can see what works and amend any material which informal and formal feedback may show needs modification.

However, there were concerns about the need to improve communication between the course designers and writers at the centre, and the tutors who were teaching the course in the regions. For example, the need to modify the tutor component, where the distance teaching component had not achieved the objectives set for it, had led to examples of the text materials being used as a resource for tutors rather than as a set of self-standing materials.

Some tutors were critical of the distance learning texts. For example, they questioned the accuracy of the content of the materials and they were critical about the way in which materials were intended to be used. The reason for the problems was perceived as being that the central materials' developers neither appeared to welcome feedback on errors and nor did the developers deliver material themselves to trainees. Tutors, therefore, felt that they ought to be involved themselves in the production of distance learning materials. However, while they had access to the production facilities necessary to produce their own resources, they felt they did not have adequate time to prepare such material.

Inland Revenue was undergoing major structural changes at the time of the research (1994), so the situation described could well have been temporary (Case Study 6.1). However, it does serve to highlight clearly the tensions which can exist between the different stakeholders who take responsibility for different elements of training provision, and also the vital need for ongoing communication and collaboration between the different parties to ensure the delivery of relevant, up-to-date, targeted training.

Course content and skills

The courses included in our research covered a range of different types of learning skills taught through OFL. These included GCSE maths, management and supervisory skills, machine operations, retail assistant training, information technology training, and specialists training for complex clerical skills (Post Office). On the whole, the evidence for the effectiveness of OFL in teaching these sometimes very different skills was positive. There were three areas in particular, however, where there appeared to be conflicting opinions among the tutors involved.

1. The suitability of a hierarchical subject like maths for teaching through open and flexible methods. This was questioned by several tutors. Two concerns in particular were mentioned. One was whether hierarchical subjects such as maths could be taught on a flexible basis when a core concept might be missed. The response to this problem at the college concerned was to repeat certain key modules for those who joined the course at different times of the year. Those colleges who operated a maths workshop in support of students who worked through self-study materials did not have this particular problem. However, students nevertheless had limited access to the workshop if they were working full time and were undertaking what was essentially distance study with timetabled tutor support. Ideally, tutors would like to see such students have some form of access to tutorial help as and when it is needed. The other concern identified was in the need for regular feedback and assessment of progress with such a subject. Again, at Plymouth, the self-study system in operation used a considerable amount of self-assessment material. However, it was clear from feedback from the students that some induction to using self-study materials such as help and guidance about the purpose and use of self-assessment material would be useful.

2. The problem of how best to use open and flexible methods when machine skills were being taught. This was raised by tutors on such a course. Their particular concern was that the video in use did not appear to give the students a sufficiently accurate 'feel' of the machine they were going to handle subsequently. However, it was also recognized that the problem might be one of the quality and appropriateness of the video material itself. Certainly, the intention with this particular problem was to try to move on to multimedia applications in the expectation that this would be better at meeting the particular teaching needs of the tutors. There was also a problem associated with the course organization model in which the video was sent to the students prior to their attendance at the residential workshop to enable them to prepare for the tutor-led component. It had been noted by the tutors that students had not necessarily been able to take time out from their normal work duties in order to undertake the preparatory work in as detailed a manner as was planned, even though arrangements for overtime payments had been made.

3. The appropriateness of open and flexible approaches in the area of person skills. This was the third type of skills about which tutors expressed some doubt. By person skills here, they were talking about group skills, interviewing skills, management skills and so on. It should be noted, however, that the concern was expressed in relation to a certain type of distance or independent learning package, namely those which were complete learning packages undertaken in a self-study setting with no tutorial or group support.

Open and flexible approaches were seen as essential in situations involving recall of information. The issue of retention was raised by tutors unprompted. Their concern was with the need to try to get students to apply their learning as soon as possible. The advantages on the flexible course, of being able to reflect on their learning in relation to their own work practice while they were actually at work rather than having just to remember the material through the traditionally taught block release course, was seen as a considerable benefit. One example came from the Post Office Counters' course for agency staff, where open and flexible materials were used both for initial training and as a back-up for 'refresher' training on those work problems which were relatively infrequent. The view was that those aspects of the work, which staff had to deal with on a daily basis, could be relatively easily learned and reinforced through constant practice. However, those problems which only arise infrequently staff were unlikely to remember accurately how to handle. In such situations, the appropriate open and flexible materials were available to them in order to ensure that correct procedures were followed.

In contrast, the use of open and flexible approaches' materials for preparatory work, prior to a tutor-led session, was reported by a number of tutors to be a generally less than satisfactory approach. This was, in part, because the material was often 'information heavy' and, in part, because the necessary time for study during working hours was frequently difficult to find.

The learner approach to training

It has been shown in a number of studies that students learn as well through open and flexible learning as they do in traditional learning (Moore, 1990). However, further studies report quite unequivocally that different types of students or trainees do better than others with different forms of provision. Some reasons which contribute to the success of individual students in distance, open or flexible learning which are suggested from findings in other studies include the student's readiness for self-directed learning, their competence with study skills, maturity, motivation and previous experience of different types of learning provision.

When it comes to examining the learning effectiveness of different types of provision, the literature does not seem to acknowledge the necessarily differential nature of the process and outcomes for different types of learners. Taken together, what the many different studies are actually telling us is that different forms of provision are differentially effective, and that all can be improved. That is, any particular kind of provision will be more effective with some students than it will be with others. Different types of students will learn more effectively with some forms of provision than with others. Pask has shown that serialist learners learn more effectively from material which is structured in a serialist manner (Pask, 1988). Similarly Entwistle and Tait have shown that students with a particular study orientation are likely to define effective teaching in ways which reflect their own orientation (Entwistle and Tait, 1990).

The fact that alternative forms of provision are differentially effective for different types of student means that if a distance, open or flexible learning mode of provision is adopted, some students, who would previously have been among the beneficiaries of the traditional system, will be among the losers under the alternative approach. Often this can be hidden among the overall 'wastage' figures.

In particular, resource-based learning resulted in student problems with study skills, with students reluctant to take the initiative in accessing tutors and with student workload. The danger of a self-paced system becoming a no-paced one is also acknowledged, with the consequent need for checkpoints and deadlines to be set by teaching staff. The demands made of staff on the new course were very different from those on the course presented in the conventional way. The need by students for personal attention, plenty of tutor contact and explanation was described as 'paramount'.

The early identification of students and trainees most likely to benefit, and most likely to lose from the adoption of alternative forms of provision, is clearly crucial. However, in spite of the strides forward in our understanding of learning processes, we are still a long way off from being able to do this. We have yet to learn how to balance the different components which might contribute to effective learning through distance, open or flexible teaching and training programmes. So, for instance, the 'maturity' to which Lewis refers that students, who are faced with the challenge of open learning appear to develop (Lewis, 1983), may actually be displaying the confidence, commitment and competence in a particular learning situation which Pratt (1988) argues is necessary for successful autonomous and self-directing learners (Pratt, 1988). It may also be, as Hawkridge (1994) claims, that 'Younger trainees are more likely to succeed with [technology based training] than older ones less familiar with the technology'.

Critical issues arising in the implementation of open learning programmes

Implementation of open learning programmes

This looks at different examples of training practice which are firmly grounded in the day-to-day realities of company life. By exploring how different companies have actually responded to a range of training problems and dilemmas we can identify lessons learnt from a broad range of training experiences and the implications for the successful implementation of open and flexible approaches to training.

City and Guilds Process Plant Operations

Hull College of FE provides a course on City and Guilds Process Plant Operations for BP employers. The key features of the course are:

- the students (all male) are aged between 19 and 50 and have few educational qualifications. Also, many of them are employed on a shift-work basis
- the course is based on text materials, and consists of a file of print material for each module studied, together with formative assessment

- supervision is provided on site on a weekly basis, with tutors available for four hours every Friday
- the students are expected to work in their own time, and are not given any time off work other than for meetings and seminars with their tutors.

The key problems encountered in implementing the course relate to two key factors. Firstly, the students had limited prior educational experience, and secondly, the fact that students are required to study in their own time. For example, when the course was first introduced between 20 and 30 per cent of students never completed their first module, and the college and the company both agreed that the biggest problem for students was that of self-discipline. A number of different methods were adopted in order to address these concerns, such as:

- in-depth counselling about the problems of studying through open learning
- aims are clearly set with strict targets and deadlines, and progress is strictly monitored
- employer sanctions are available if there is lack of progress. For example, if the college is concerned about a student's progress, a letter is sent to the BP training department for them to take up the problem with the student. If progress continues to be a problem, employer support is withdrawn and the student will have to pay for their own materials
- the tutor role was viewed as crucial in providing support and countering any feelings of isolation that the students may experience. However, the tutors feel that the limited contact which they have with the students may mean that support may not be available when the students need them.

One of the key strengths of open learning in this context was that it enabled shift workers to participate in learning, and also that the experience of this method of learning would contribute to preparation for lifelong learning. However, stakeholders in this scheme felt that more emphasis on positive incentives, such as providing study time within working hours, providing facilities such as study rooms to create a better learning environment, and also providing ongoing access to tutor support, are clearly required so that students are positively motivated and supported in their learning.

Certificate in Personnel Practice

Plymouth College of FE provides a course leading to a Certificate in Personnel Practice, which is offered to two very distinct sets of customers. Firstly, there is a block course for MOD service people, which runs for five weeks and the flexible learning for personnel at more junior levels, which runs for nine months. This course, therefore, provides valuable insights into strengths and weakness of different approaches, for while the course content is virtually identical in both courses, there are major differences in approaches to the subject.

The key features of the flexible course are:

- the students are usually in full-time work, and have day-release to attend workshops of 2 to 4 days' duration over a nine-month period

- the work programme is designed around the workplace, for example workbooks are completed in relation to work practices
- there is a mentoring scheme whereby an individual in the company acts as a mentor to the student within the organization and provides feedback to the college
- evaluation relates the quality and value of the programme against performance at work.

The key features of the block course are:

- students come from across the country, and they are in the process of changing careers
- students cover nine months' part-time work in five full-time weeks – it is, therefore, a highly intensive course
- students do not get the opportunity to apply learning to the workplace
- it is not possible to relate evaluation to work performance, which relates instead to student results and opinions of the course.

The central drawbacks of the block course are seen as being that students have no opportunity to relate their learning to work practices, and also that there is no time or space for them to reflect on the issues. A critical finding which emerged from a comparison of these two courses was that the students on the block course were used to didactic teaching and, therefore, had certain expectations about the style of instruction which should be used. Course tutors attributed this to their background in the services:

> Throughout their careers they have been instructed to do this or that and they find it a culture shock when they come here and are taught in a completely different way, so I think most of the tutors tend to teach them some of it quite didactically and some of it is more informal, they definitely can't handle suddenly going from one extreme to another.

However, it was also pointed out that the time constraints meant that the course had to be structured in such a way that students did not have sufficient time to reflect upon the issues. Also, there were the difficulties that students encounter in subjects where there are 'no hard and fast answers' and that for this target group, they should be addressed within the course. The college view was that while the five-week course did have serious drawbacks, it was seen as meeting a need which could otherwise not be met. The problems encountered, although recognized, were therefore accepted as a price which had to be paid. Possible options for improvement would be to counsel students on different learning processes, and also incorporate some preparatory work on different learning styles, which could help students to reflect not just on course content but also on the process of learning.

Inland Revenue – management training

The foundation management course is for first-line managers, ie those who super-vise clerks and is seen as a six-month course. It consists of four distance education texts and three periods of residential training, which last a week. Course materials are seen as carrying the main content, and tutorial sessions aim to develop further the learners understanding of the materials.

The key features are:

- course participants encompass a wide range of experience of working with the Inland Revenue and different motivations for undertaking the course. Trainees vary from new entrants with minimal qualifications through to highly experienced staff who have recently been promoted
- prior to each residential period, participants are sent the relevant materials to prepare for the residential component.

The concerns are:

- there are conflicts between the demands on trainees' time to do the distance component and the needs of the workplace offices. People are, therefore, frequently unable to do the preparatory work for the course
- individual progress on the course varies considerably

Rank Xerox – self-study packages

The training aim at Rank Xerox is that each employee receives 40 hours of training and development each year. Training is provided in a number of different ways, and the method under consideration here is the open learning self-study package, which is available for a range of topics such as Word for Windows and other technical training courses. The courses also vary in length from 8–40 hours, and the aim here is to identify key features and issues arising when self-study packages are used across a spectrum of training needs.

The key features of the self-study package are:

- open learning courses consist of self-contained independent learning packages designed to be studied independently by 'delegates' (the term used by Rank Xerox)
- individual members of staff select the mode of study they prefer
- when delegates decide to undertake an open learning programme, they visit their open learning centre and agree a date to start the training, and a learning contract is drawn up
- there is no tutor support available with the self-study packages.

The concerns are:

- it is difficult to monitor individual's progress
- it is easy for training to take second place
- motivation for sustaining study can be a problem, particularly when the delegate has a heavy workload
- the attitude of line managers is crucial in helping delegates to sustain study. However, some line managers still see open learning as 'reading a book when you should be working'.

There was strong consensus within Rank Xerox that there is likely to be a major growth in open learning within the company. A major benefit of the open learning package was seen to be that they allowed self-pacing, the downside of this being the motivation problem. The availability of open learning centres where delegates could study in peace was seen as very important for the success of open learning. Also, it was felt that open learning could be integrated into the work situation in a more immediate way.

Common themes and concerns

A number of common themes and concerns arise in the company practices described, which are viewed as the key to success in the provision of open learning. From these various experiences we can, therefore, identify a common set of critical factors, which are linked to the successful implementation of open learning.

The most common problem identified in association with open learning programmes was that of motivation, and this was linked to three key factors. Firstly, younger students and those with limited educational experiences had initial difficulty in coping with the open learning format. Secondly, the more self-pacing the systems were, the more students encountered problems in sustaining their study, and thirdly, poor levels of organizational support (in terms of providing adequate time and space for study, and also in terms of line manager support) were identified as critical factors in student motivation. For example it was clearly shown that the expectation that students would do initial preparatory study in their own time was highly unrealistic and, therefore, unsuccessful.

A number of methods were, therefore, employed to tackle the problem of motivation, and the most successful programmes are those that combine a range of methods, which together provide adequate support to the student. These methods fall into three broad categories:

- direct student support
- structured learning programmes
- workplace support.

The Safeway Management Training Programme (see Chapter 4) provides an example of training practice, which combines the key elements of successful open learning. For example, there was a strong consensus among Safeway staff that the new training approach, combining the use of workbooks, hands-on experience and close supervision, provided practical relevant and effective training programmes. As one management trainee described the programme:

> This is the most structured programme I have seen, areas of responsibility are given to people, there are constant reviews to check that you are happy and that we have input into training and to make sure we're going in the right direction (Calder *et al.*, 1995).

Some of the methods identified in the research in order to provide direct student support included for example:

- counselling prior to study and available throughout study
- negotiation of learning contracts and timetables for study
- access to tutorial help.

The literature available on open learning strongly reinforces the findings here that readily accessible student support services are a fundamental component in open learning programmes (Scriven, 1991; Warren, 1994). Of central concern is the individual learner's needs and the corresponding support services which are required as these will directly influence learning effectiveness.

In Moss' (1991) study of a flexible learning initiative for sixth formers, he highlights the problems encountered by students in the 16–19 age group, and suggests that for younger students entering into open and flexible learning programmes, tutor support and study skills should be available for all students. Also Baxter's (1990) findings in his comparative study of a conventional and a resource-based course hold important ramifications for meeting learner needs, for he found that the two types of delivery generated different study problems. For example, in the conventional programme, the key problems were in the area of lectures and student assessment whereas in the resource-based programme the key problem areas lay in use of reference materials and with tutorials.

Ongoing tutor support is viewed as a key feature of student support services, and as we have seen in the examples here, access to tutor support is often limited and this creates problems for students. There is, therefore, a need for companies and training providers alike to recognize the central importance of tutor support in open learning programmes. As Fricker (cited in Paine, 1988) tells us:

> The role of the tutor in open learning is vastly different from the comparable role in most traditional forms of training. Many tutors are required to play a complex and all-encompassing role which demands a greater number of skills compared with that of the traditional trainer.

In terms of the need to provide structured programmes, some of the key characteristics of structured programmes include:

- aims clearly set with strict targets
- regular feedback and assessment of students' work
- monitoring of progress (which is a major challenge in self-paced programmes)
- high-quality learning materials
- appropriate and relevant course content.

In terms of workplace support, key issues which were identified include:

- line manager support
- adequate time within work to study

- a suitable learning environment is provided such as a study room
- the opportunity for and guidance in applying learning to work, and reflecting on learning in relation to work.

Again the literature on open learning serves to reinforce the findings in our study (Bailey; Fricker; cited in Paine, 1988). Bailey, for example, argues that there are three basic rationales for providing guidance in work-based open learning and these are

- to strengthen the learner's motivation
- to improve the relevance of learning
- to improve the quality of learning.

The need for close integration of work practice and training, and for guidance within the workplace, highlights the crucial and difficult role of line managers within the training process:

> Workplace supervisors and managers have key roles to play in open learning. Where previously they granted day release and checked progress, a relatively passive role, their open learning roles are more active and often linked to new quality aspirations by the organization (Bailey, cited in Paine, 1988).

In relation to learner needs in company training, then the role of the line manager is crucial and this in turn highlights the need for line manager training 'in training' so that they can carry out their roles effectively.

The examples in these case studies of some of the problems typically encountered in open learning highlight the changing and more demanding roles for staff associated with training. They strongly reinforce the need for clarity regarding the training roles and responsibilities of line managers, tutors and training providers, and the need for collaboration between them in order to ensure that while the learning process is integral to the workplace, it does not get lost within it.

Chapter 7

Critical issues

This final chapter considers the issues, which present both the greatest challenges and the greatest opportunities to training problems and the potential of open and distance learning to offer solutions to those problems. Open and distance solutions to training problems are by no means the global panacea which is often claimed. Nevertheless, their effect on the development of creative solutions has been much greater and far-reaching than simply the addition of new and alternative modes of delivery. There has been a need to involve more stakeholders in a greater variety of ways, a need to understand learning and the complex ways in which circumstances interact with provision, and a willingness by training and education professionals to change roles and patterns of work. The future will, of necessity, make even greater demands on all stakeholders in the provision of education and training through open and flexible learning.

Introduction

The search for a solution to the lack of appropriately skilled workers by both government and employers continues. While the perception of vocational education and training as the key to economic problems appears to be shared across all countries and cultures, the locus of responsibility for its provision, and the quality and appropriateness of that provision varies. In the UK there are concerns about the low levels of training generally but the training and development needs of the most needy group – basic operatives and craft grades of workers – are relatively neglected. There appears to be very little existing provision indeed. Some years ago, the situation *vis-à-vis* the mismatch between the substantial amount of adult learning, which was actually taking place in private compared to the relatively small amount showing up in formal public provision, led to the introduction of the term 'the adult learning iceberg'. In relation to the training and development of basic operatives and craft level staff – the security guards, cleaners, care workers, warehouse workers, assembly line workers, clerical staff – the term which comes to mind is 'the empty shell'. The appearance of provision and activity is often there, but in reality, and with a few splendid exceptions such as those we have referred to in our case studies, there is little if any real activity behind the rhetoric and fine plans.

In part, the problem lies with the way in which the situation is often presented and discussed. All the stakeholders in vocational education and training, and in open and distance provision, share a common environment. Thus, governments, large companies, small and medium enterprises, communications media organizations, public training providers, private providers, schools and trade unions all have to cope with the same national and international economic, social, political and technological uncertainties. However, while some of the stakeholder groups see themselves as relatively powerless and limited to responding to the environment, other stakeholders both respond to and create the environment within which they operate.

Who do we mean when we talk of employers?

For example when we talk of 'employers' we can be talking about an organization which consists simply of a self-employed person, such as the owner of a corner shop, who hires occasional help, or a global company controlling more wealth than do many independent countries. Focusing first on global companies, there is a clear tension between the interests of a national economy and its labour market and the workforce needs of large multinationals.

Following the statement that... Global companies were seeking the greatest relative competitive advantage and were shifting the location of their operations to achieve that goal, Sir Ron Dearing commented

> Those companies are footloose. They are conscious of where world growth is, where the lowest costs can be achieved. They are very aware of what is happening in South America, India and China... Since the companies are mobile, what attracts them is the quality of the people... So what we have to create is a society whose members are committed to learning throughout life (Carvel, 1997a).

Some idea of the extent of the power now wielded by global companies can be gathered from the proportion of the world's wealth which they now control.

> ... the largest 500 companies now control 42 per cent of the world's wealth. Of the biggest 100 economies, half are now corporations and half are countries... just 250 companies in Britain take almost half of everything we spend... Twelve of the world's most important industries – including...

electronics, computers, media – are each more than 40 per cent dominated by five or fewer corporations (Vidal, 1997).

There is no single source of information about the total number of companies in the UK, nor of their sizes. However, a Department of Trade and Industry (DTI) report on small firms refers to 3.6 million enterprises in the UK, of which only 5 per cent employ 10 or more employees (Hillman, 1996). Other estimates suggest that approximately 50 per cent of all employed people in the UK work for companies with fewer than 100 employees (see Table 7.1).

Table 7.1 *Distribution of company size by proportion of workforce employed in the UK (1991)*

Company size	Number of companies 000's	%	Proportion of UK workforce %	cumulative %
1–2	1735	64	11	
3–5	565	21	10	21
6–10	196	7	7	28
11–19	97	4	6	34
20–49	65	2	9	43
50–99	20	1	7	50
100–199	10	1	8	58
200–499	6	–	9	67
500–999	2	–	6	73
1,000+	1	–	27	100
Total	2697	100	100	

Source: adapted from Storey (1994)

The reason this is important is that reports of training provision by companies inevitably refer to 'employers' as if they were a homogeneous group of organizations. Even when the figures are broken down, it is usually into different employment sectors rather than different size sectors. The problem with this approach is that the training patterns of small firms have a disproportionate effect on the overall picture. For example, 64 per cent of businesses employ only one or two people, who together make up only 11 per cent of the workforce. Some studies deal with this dilemma by only reporting on companies with 100 employees or more. However, this can produce just as much distortion the other way, in that there is substantial evidence which suggests that the training patterns of small businesses are very different from those of the medium and large employers.

It should be pointed out that there is no single definition of a small firm, although the European Commission has coined the term 'small and medium enterprise' (SME). This sector comprises three groups (Storey, 1994):

- micro enterprises containing between 0 and 9 employees

- small enterprises with between 10 and 99 employees
- medium enterprises with between 100 and 499 employees.

There are problems with defining companies simply in terms of their size as different sectors have different perceptions of what constitutes a small business. But, for the purposes of training needs and provision, size is clearly a key measure. Certainly in the UK, one of the most consistent criticisms of small companies over the past few years has been their apparent reluctance to invest in training their workers.

> … in general, small firms are much less likely either to provide training or to have a training plan. Medium and large sized organizations (100 employees or more) constitute only 0.5 per cent of the 3.6 million enterprises in the UK (95 per cent of which have fewer than 10 employees)… (Hillman, 1996).

Both US and UK research clearly suggests that large employers provide more formal training than do small employers (Storey, 1994). Other evidence suggests smaller firms may to some extent compensate by providing informal training to employees while they are with the company (Curran *et al.*, cited in Storey, 1994). This view is supported by other more recent research which suggests that over 75 per cent of UK companies are actively involved in training (Crequer, 1997b). A study undertaken for the former Department of Employment found that the majority of training is 'on the job', with only half of all worksites providing any form of 'off-the-job' training, whether on- or off-site (NOP [1992]).

The same study also showed that smaller companies were 'considerably less likely to be aware of Open Learning than organizations employing over 100 people' (NOP [1992]); with awareness of open learning among firms employing between 6 and 10 people being only 34 per cent, rising to 75 per cent among organizations employing more than 100 people. Clearly, if an employer is unaware of the availability of training opportunities, then it is unlikely that they will take advantage of them. Local Training and Enterprise Councils were set up, in part to try to provide a solution to this problem, but again, small businesses were far less likely to be aware of or to use their local TECS than were the larger companies (NOP [1992]).

There is some evidence that the reluctance of small firms to train 'may as much reflect employees' attitudes as employers' (Storey, 1994). Other commentators have also commented on this phenomenon.

> There is a mutual and self-destructive compact between the unskilled worker and the firm, in which it makes sense neither for the individual to invest time in training nor for the firm to offer it. As with so much else in the British system, the blind lead the blind. A teenager has to be very long-sighted indeed to want to undertake training that will raise his or her lifetime earnings only after the age of thirty-five and which, although it may help reduce the likelihood of unemployment, is for any individual an impossible risk to assess. At the same time firms are under pressure to maximize short-term profits,

and incurring immediate costs for uncertain future benefits is equally irra-
tional. In any case there is no certainty that the trained workers will stay with
the firm that shoulders the costs. The rational approach, in terms of the
system, is to minimize training and poach the skilled when market conditions
demand it (Hutton, 1996).

The question raised here is the lack of any evidence, which shows a clear financial
benefit to employees in small companies who do undertake training. Indeed, Storey,
in a review of the topic reported that 'there does not appear to be any thorough
empirical study which demonstrates that the provision of training either by, or for,
a small firm clearly leads to better performance of that firm' (Storey, 1994).

Workforce attitudes

While we argued earlier that the multinationals are now recognizing the importance
of the stakeholder approach and its implications for generic as well as specific
training, the apparent lack of incentives for small companies to invest in training of
any kind means that responsibility for training often falls on employees themselves.
In a discussion of the issue some years ago, Woodcock (1991) commented that 'We
have to decide to whom the training belongs – the company or the individual – and
the answer is the individual because he/she can take their skills where they wish.
Thus there is no incentive for companies to train to a point beyond their own
particular needs'.

Howevever, employees' attitudes to training in general, regardless of the mode in
which it is offered, is complex and, to a considerable extent, reflects their attitudes
to their employer as well as to their own prospects. There is evidence that for many
people, even their understanding of the term 'training' is different from the one
understood by employers and by training professionals. Campanelli *et al.* (1994) for
example report that:

> 'proper' training activity was seen by many to imply the presence and contri-
> bution of a (qualified) trainer. Reading of manuals and other forms of
> self-teaching were not generally seen to be in the same category. Associated
> with this was in some cases an implicit assumption that training is something
> that is provided for (or even imposed upon) the individual employees, rather
> than something which he or she undertakes on a personal initiative. 'Self-
> training' was considered to be a separate concept from 'training' and activities
> undertaken purely for pleasure did not generally constitute 'training'.

Although one interpretation here might be that learners do not see self-teaching as
proper training, in our own study, learners were quite clear about the similarities
and differences between 'traditional' teaching and open and flexible learning.
However, the key issue in the statement above centres on the apparent reluctance
by people to see training as something which can be undertaken on a personal

initiative. Clearly, this has quite profound implications for those who wish to extend training opportunities. The comment has been made that 'Training is an infrastructure investment like roads, rail, health and the environment. If you don't invest in training, then you can't make the most of the new technology the economy so desperately needs' (Woodcock, 1991).

It appears, however, that the purpose of the proposed training may play a greater role in its acceptance by potential trainees than previously thought. For example induction training, to enable recruits to do the job, appears to be well recognized and accepted as a useful and necessary activity. Similarly, courses which are part of an established personal development route towards future promotion attract trainees relatively easily. Where problems seem to occur is where there is a change of policy on training by the employer. In effect, there appears to be a lack of trust on the part of many employees about the possible motives behind employer-led training initiatives (see Case Study 7.1).

Case Study 7.1: Severn Trent Water

For example, at Severn Trent Water, it was decided to introduce NVQs for all existing 3,000 craft and process workers, with new staff expected to achieve the appropriate levels within an agreed time-limit. 'Many staff did not at first see why they needed a qualification to do a job they had been doing for years. The "cost" to the individual was their fear and concern about what was seen initially as a potential threat – these developments were taking place against a delicate background of privatization and cutbacks in the workforce'.

Source: Calder and Newton (1995)

The reasons for this lack of trust are not hard to find. As mentioned in Chapter 1, changes in patterns of employment over the past two decades have all been to the disadvantage of the most vulnerable members of the workforce.

The shift towards part-time employment (Boseley, 1994) noted in Chapter 1 is just one example of the way in which changes in the patterns of employment are affecting the pattern of training.

> The Post Office chairman emphasized that at a time when people were being forced to change their jobs more often than before, the challenge for the NCVQ was to create a situation where people became accustomed to a different work ethic.
>
> Mr Heron said: 'We are part of a society where nobody can any more be guaranteed a job for life. So we have to ensure that the qualifications we are offering give people 'life-long employability' (Harper, 1994).

The temporary nature of many jobs, the lengthening hours of work for both men and women and the general culture of 'downsizing' and 'outsourcing' mean that insecure staff, the newly redundant and the long-term unemployed may find it difficult to concentrate on planning the training that may be so vital to the future of the economy.

> In the labour market the 'contract' culture has become more entrenched, spreading fears about job insecurity, while a growing number of firms relocate their manufacturing production to low-cost developing countries (Hutton, 1996).

New patterns of work involve little or no continuity of career while demanding multiskilling for maximum labour market flexibility.

> The other elements in the newly insecure category are growing explosively. Paul Gregg of the London School of Economics computes that temporary work has grown by a quarter since 1992, and nearly three-quarters of male manual workers have experienced cuts in real wages over the same period. As for the bottom 30 per cent – the unemployed or those working for poverty wages – by 1995 19.1 per cent of all British households of working age had no adult in work. The gap between them and the newly insecure is widening (Hutton, 1996).

The solutions tried by successful managers to overcome the problems presented by this environment, when they wish to introduce new and innovative training schemes, are many and varied. They include careful planning ahead with well-publicized pilot schemes, full involvement of the unions at all stages, realistic timetabling for pilot schemes to allow problems to emerge and be dealt with; and involvement of local managers and training staff from the start so that they 'own' the scheme sufficiently to encourage and support staff who are taking part.

Front-line training providers

The problematic environment faced by trainees and potential trainees is also shared by the training providers. Again, a critical issue here has been the suspicion and sometimes fear which has been felt when changes have been introduced by 'management'. In the case of further education in the UK, national front page headlines such as 'Colleges too broke to educate properly' (Thomson, 1997) underline the cumulative pressures with which the sector has been coping. The recognition of the very real educational benefits to be gained from open, distance and flexible approaches is dissipated in the quite valid concern that simple cost saving is the driving force behind the official enthusiasm for these new methods. At the same time, the ever present threat of the outsourcing of in-company training, and of competition for FE sector provision from private providers, ensures that any innovatory projects which carry even a slight risk of failure will be unlikely to be either promoted or adopted unless there are clear potential cost benefits.

The attitudes of management level training providers are some considerable distance away from the front-line training providers. While the former may embrace open, flexible and distance provision as a welcome solution to cost and staffing problems, the latter see only too clearly the personal implications of the savings being made. While many of the front-line staff do recognize the economic constraints under which their organization must work, and attempt to reskill themselves in the development and use of these newer forms of training approaches and technologies as preparation for a future which has arrived, others remain to be convinced of the educational benefits.

If the front line of training providers are to be active players on the field rather than remaining on the sidelines as frustrated non-players, then some crucial preparatory work needs to be undertaken.

---

1. Increase awareness – of what open courses, learning packages and self-study materials are available and where to get appropriate information about them.

2. Increase understanding – of how different media can be used to meet training needs, and of the potential of different approaches for solving training problems.

3. Increase ownership – of which packages and materials are used, and of modifications introduced as improvements to materials.

Firstly, there is a lack of awareness about relevant good quality open and distance learning materials and programmes among providers. Awareness about reliable unbiased sources of clear and up-to-date information on what is available urgently needs to be raised.

Secondly, there is little in-service training of trainers about the strengths, limitations and uses of open, flexible and distance provision for different sorts of learner. For example there still appears to be a widespread assumption that manual skills cannot be taught via distance methods, or that basic grade workers do not have the study skills to undertake open learning in spite of many successful examples.

Thirdly, for people who are used to an active teaching role, there is little advice on the changes in role needed for successful adoption and implementation of open, flexible and distance methods of training. At the same time there is frequently little opportunity for trainers to acquire ownership of courses designed and produced elsewhere. Even opportunities for feedback to course developers to improve the materials can be limited, if not actually non-existent.

Whose needs is the government meeting?

The critical issues for the government relate to the need for a clear sense of direction and purpose for both vocational education and training, and for the adoption and further dissemination of open, flexible and distance solutions to training problems.

Numerous commentators have drawn attention to the need for a comprehensible and unambiguous policy which could underpin strategic planning and provide firm guidelines for the establishment of priorities. Primary among the considerations which such a policy should address is the issue of who owns the training? In other words who is the client?

1. Is the primary client the individual who is to be trained? If this is the case, then the aim of the training would be to meet the needs, aims and expectations of the individual. In other words, the purpose of the training would be determined by the potential trainee, whether already employed or unemployed. The issue then is the extent and quality of the advice and support to the individual on the choice of subjects and the skills they would need to acquire for their own purposes, and the most appropriate method, provider, timing and cost of training
2. Is the primary client the employer? Is it all types and sizes of employers in all sectors, or do the needs of particular categories of employer take precedence? Are the different employers explicit about their needs and the criteria they are using in assessing their workforce needs. Are they aiming for competitive advantage through cost reduction and efficiency or through new developments and innovatory products for new markets?
3. Is the primary client the wider society? Are the aims to have full employment, or to maximize gross national product? Is society willing to pay for training and education, or is it seen as a commodity which should be purchased directly by the customers and paid for as and when it is used? Are individuals and employers willing to give precedence to the needs of society over their own particular training and education needs?

Realistically, the primary client is unlikely to be the individual, or even employers as such, even though both would be likely to benefit. The real answer is likely to be some sort of mix, which increasingly will include other stakeholders, ranging from international agencies such as the World Bank, media and telecommunications conglomerates and regional economic groupings such as the European Community, to local communities attempting to attract employment into the area, and other groups trying to tackle the social problems associated with long-term unemployment. It would appear that what is wanted is a motivated flexible multi-skilled workforce willing to move in and out of jobs at little notice, and to train and retrain in skills likely to attract incoming investment. General skills would be needed for maximum flexibility, but specific skills would be acquired when with a particular employer. All this at minimum cost and maximum effectiveness.

Conclusion

There is always a ready audience for simple elegant solutions to complex problems. Unfortunately, experience tells us that solutions to complex problems are themselves usually complex, particularly if people are involved. Contingency theory offers one explanation for why we find getting the right solution so problematic. The idea that there is such a thing as 'one best approach' is rejected, and is instead replaced by the 'view that the structure and operation of an organization is dependent ("contingent") on the situational variables it faces – the main ones being environment, technology and size' (Burnes, 1996). Although there are serious criticisms of this theory, primarily in attempts to apply its ideas 'logically' and 'scientifically', it is useful in that it does highlight the importance of context. Regardless of whether we are looking at the national level, the organizational level or at the level of the individual, what this theory is essentially saying is that in looking for solutions, we need to be sufficiently flexible and sufficiently confident to choose the solutions which best meet the needs and the situational variables which are current.

In trying to disentangle the reality from the training and open learning rhetoric, three aspects in particular have emerged as holding the key to the virtuous circle of successful education and training.

---

1. What should be taught – the range of areas of knowledge and the skills which are taught to trainees?

2. Who should be taught?

3. In what form the provision should be made available?

The issue of what subjects and skills should be taught is problematic for several reasons. Training of employed workers for current jobs involves the teaching of knowledge and skills which can be immediately applied, or at least where it is intended to apply them in the near future. Similarly, the training of employed workers for future work, say at a higher level, in a field which is linked to their current field of employment still holds relevance. It is possible for the participants in the training to see how the knowledge and skills are applied. There may even be opportunities to try out or practise the skills being acquired, and the knowledge is likely to add to their current understanding. The problem arises when people are being trained for jobs which, for them, do not currently exist. Unemployed people who are trained in basic computer skills before returning to unemployment are unlikely to have acquired study skills, or indeed any skills which will stay with them for long unless they are utilized within a short period of time. Training is not simply the process of acquiring knowledge and skills, but must also contain the opportunity to apply, and continue to apply the knowledge and the skills so painfully acquired. Neither will simply providing training in the subject areas available, that is in the subject areas for which provision exists, meet any real needs. In an age of performance indicators, numbers of courses provided often obscure the dubious relevance of those courses to anyone's needs.

When we turn to the question of who should receive training, again there are likely to be continuing problems for basic grade staff and the unemployed. The aim behind the UK committee who produced the Kennedy Report was to widen participation in further education. Among its major recommendations were a number aimed at widening the demand for learning. We have seen how those who already have education and training go on to undertake more (Kennedy, 1997). In part, this is facilitated by the increasing expectation among employers that their managers and other middle and higher grades of staff undertake regular updating and refresher courses as a matter of routine. This needs also to be the expectation for basic grade staff. We did come across some examples of updating and refresher training of existing basic grade staff, but this was relatively unusual, and tended to be found in organizations with a large proportion of such staff. The long-term unemployed remain the problematic group. The combination of work experience with training appears to be one type of solution, rather than them being offered as alternatives. However, the cooperation of business and industry is needed for this, and to date, again with a few key exceptions, their support for such ventures has been hard won by local colleges.

It is in considering the ways in which training might be offered that we start to complete the circle. The importance of work-based experience to accompany the training of the unemployed has already been referrred to. As we found in our own study, the knowledge already exists about how to construct and provide high-quality open, flexible and distance programmes. Training programmes using well-constructed course material, supported closely by mentors and by staff with training in assessment, together with regular monitoring of progress and feedback to course designers to improve the course, are already in operation. Associations such as the British Association of Open Learning (BAOL), and centres such as the International Centre for Distance Education (ICDL) are increasingly effective in disseminating information about training opportunities through open and distance learning. However, in many ways the task has hardly begun. The changing role of human resource development work, and the increasingly important role played by line managers and by Jobcentre advisers in negotiating training needs with individuals, means that a rapidly widening pool of people need some understanding of the options available, together with the strengths and weaknesses of different types of courses, using different types of approaches. It also means that education and training is no longer the reponsibility of a few professionals, but, increasingly, of the wider community.

References

Argyris, C and Schön, D (1978) *Organisational Learning: A theory of Action Perspective*, Addison-Wesley, Reading, Mass.

Bailey, E P (1993) 'Open learning: a quantum leap: a conference organised by the National Extension College and the Careers Research Advisory Council', *Open Learning* (February), 53–4.

Bates, A W (1991) 'Third generation distance education: the challenge of new technology', *Research in Distance Education* 3 (2), 10–15.

Bates, A W (1995) *Technology, Open learning and Distance Education*, Routledge, London.

Baxter, E P (1990) 'Comparing conventional and resource based education in chemical engineering: student perceptions of a teaching innovation', *Higher Education* 19, 323–40.

Beinhart, S and Smith, P (1998) *National Adult Learning Survey 1997*, Research Report 49, Department for Education and Employment, Sheffield.

Berger, N O (1990) 'A qualitative study of the process of self-directed learning', in *School of Education*, Virginia Commonwealth University, Richmond, Virginia.

Blundell, R *et al.* (1996) *The Determinants and Effects of Work Related Training in Britain*, Institute for Fiscal Studies, London.

Boseley, S (1994) 'Part-time route to cutting costs', *The Guardian*, London.

Brookfield, S (1986) *Understanding and Facilitating Adult Learning*, Open University Press, Milton Keynes.

Brown, S (1997) 'Corporate context and cultural change: distance learning in BT', in S Brown, *Open and Distance Learning: Case Studies from Industry and Education*. Kogan Page, London.

Brown, S (ed) (1997) *Open and Distance Learning: Case Studies from Industry and Education*, Kogan Page, London.

Burnes, B (1996) *Managing Change: A Strategic Approach to Organisational Dynamics*, Pitman Publishing, London.

Calder, J (1993) 'Adult learning and success', in J Calder, *Disaffection and Diversity: Overcoming Barriers for Adult Learners*, Falmer Press, London.

Calder, J *et al.* (1995a) *Learning Effectiveness of Open and Flexible Learning in Vocational Education*, Research Series no. 58, Department for Education and Employment, Sheffield.

Calder, J and Newton, W (1995b) *A Study of National Vocation Qualification Achievement Through Open and Flexible Routes*, Department for Education and Employment, Sheffield.

Campanelli, P *et al.* (1994) *Training: An Exploration of the Word and the Concept with an Analysis of the Implications for Survey Design*, Employment Department, Sheffield.

Carr, R (1990) Open learning: an imprecise term, *ICDE Bulletin*, vol 22, Jan.

Carvel, J (1997) 'The artful dodger', *The Guardian*, London, *The Guardian Higher*.

Carvel, J (1997) 'Blair picks Ford for workers' university', *The Guardian*, London.

Chambers, E (1994) 'Collaborative publishing in distance education: economics and pedagogy', in G Dhanarajan, P K Ip, K S Yuen and C Swales, *Economics of Distance Education. Recent Experience*, Open Learning Institute Press, Hong Kong.

Cooper, C (1996) 'Guidance and coherence in flexible learning', in P Raggatt, R Edwards and N Small, *The Learning Society. Challenges and Trends*, Routledge, London and New York.

Cowe, R and Buckingham, L (1994) 'Britain's blinkered businesses condemned', *The Guardian*, London.

Crequer, N (1997a) 'Train or else, warn academics', *TES*, London.

Crequer, N (1997b) 'UK firms lead the way in training', *TES*, London.

Denny, C (1997) 'The split that became a lucky break', *The Guardian*, London.

Department of Employment (1990) 'Open learning, training for success in the 1990s', *Employment Gazette* (March), 138–141.

Department of Employment (1991) 'Learning how to learn', *Employment Gazette* (March), 108.

Department for Education and Employment (1996) *Lifetime Learning – a consultation document*, Department for Education and Employment, Sheffield.

Department for Education and Employment (1998) *The Learning Age: A Renaissance for a New Britain*, The Stationery Office, London.

Dhanarajan, G (1997) *Globalisation, Competitiveness and Open and Distance Education: Reflections on Quality Assurance*, Asian Association of Open Universities, Kuala Lumpur.

Doyle, P (1997) 'From the top', *The Guardian*, London.

Edwards, R (1997) *Changing Places? Flexibility, Lifelong Learning and a Learning Society*, Routledge, London and New York.

Edwards, R, Sieminski, S and Zeldin, D (eds) (1993) *Adult Learners, Education and Training*, Open University and Routledge, London.

Edwards, R et al. (1998) *Recent Thinking in Lifelong Learning: A Review of the Literature*, Department for Education and Employment, Sheffield.

Entwistle, N (1981) *Styles of Learning and Teaching*, John Wiley and Sons, Chichester.

Entwistle, N and Tait, H (1990) 'Approaches to learning, evaluations of teaching, and preferences for contrasting academic environments', *Higher Education* 19 (2), 169–94.

Farnes, N, Kornyei, I and Woodley, A (1994) *How Distance Learning Assists in the Transition Towards a Market Economy: Human Resource Development in Hungary*, European Distance Education Network (EDEN), Tallin, Estonia; EDEN Secretariat, UK.

Ford, N (1981) 'Recent Approaches to the Study and teaching of "Effective Learning" in Higher Education', *Review of Educational Research* 51 Fall, (3), 345–77.

Forrester, K et al. (1995) *Workplace Learning*, Avebury, Aldershot.

Gardner, J (1963) *Self-renewal*, Harper, Evanston, Ill.

Gooderham, P N and Hines, K (1995) 'Trends in employer-funded training as an indicator of changes in employment: the case of Norway in the 1980s', *Adult Education Quarterly* 45 (4), 213–26.

Guri-Rozenblitz, S (1993) 'Differentiating between distance/open education systems – parameters for comparison', *International Review of Education* 39 (4), 287–306.

Harper, K (1994) 'New chief qualifies his criticism of training council', *The Guardian*, London.

Harrison, R (1993) 'Disaffection and access', in J Calder, *Disaffection and Diversity: Overcoming Barriers for Adult Learners*, The Falmer Press, London.

Hawkridge, D and Hall, C (1994) 'The cost-effectiveness of technology-based training', in *THD204 Information Technology and Society Block 3 CD-ROM Disk (1995)*, The Open University, Milton Keynes.

Hawkridge, D, Newton, W et al. (1988) *Computers in company training*. Croom Helm, Beckenham, Kent.

Higgins, P (1997) 'Integrated learning in the TSB', in S Brown, *Open and Distance Learning: Case Studies from Industry and Education*, Kogan Page, London.

Hillman, J (1996) *University for Industry. Creating a National Learning Network*, Institute for Public Policy Research, London.

Hoare, S (1997) 'All change in the training field', *Times Education Supplement*, London.

Hutton, W (1996) *The State We're In*, Vintage, London.

International Centre for Distance Learning (ICDL)(1997a) *Distance Learning and Supported Open Learning UK*, Hobsons Publishing PLC, Cambridge.

ICDL (1997b) *Distance Learning and Supported Open Learning Worldwide*, Hobsons Publishing PLC, Cambridge.

Interview (1996) 'A prime concern', *Education Interface: The Apple newsletter for education in Europe* (Autumn).

Keegan, D (1996) *Foundations of Distance Education*, Routledge, London.

Keep, E (1990) 'The grass looked greener – some thoughts on the influence of comparative vocational training research on the UK policy debate', in P Ryan, *International Comparisons of Vocational Education and Training for Intermediate Skills*, Falmer Press, London.

Keep, E (1993) 'Missing, presumed skilled: training policy in the UK', in R Edwards, S Siemenski and D Zeldin, *Adult Learners, Education and Training*, Open University and Routledge, London.

Kennedy, H (1997) *Learning Works*, Further Education Funding Council, Coventry.

Kirkup, G and Jones, A (1996) 'New technologies for open learning: the superhighway to the learning society', in P Raggatt, R Edwards and N Small, *The Learning Society. Challenges and Trends*, Routledge, London and New York.

Knowles, M S (1980) *The Modern Practice of Adult Education: from Pedagogy to Andragogy* (2nd edn), Cambridge Books, New York.

Kovel-Jarvoe, P (1990) 'Organisation and administration of distance education', in M Moore, *Comtemporary Issues in American Distance Education*, Pergamon, Oxford.

Laurillard, D (1984) 'Learning from problem-solving', in F Marton, D Hounsell and N Entwistle, *The Experience of Learning*, Scottish Academic Press, Edinburgh.

Laurillard, D (1993) *Rethinking University Teaching*, Routledge, London.

Leach, R and Webb, R (1993) Opportunities through open learning, in J Calder, *Disaffection and Diversity. Overcoming Barriers for Adult Learners*, The Falmer Press, London.

Lever, M (1993) 'Informal learning opportunities and their contribution to overcoming disaffection, in J Calder, *Disaffection and Diversity. Overcoming Barriers for Adult Learners*, The Falmer Press, London.

Lewis, R (1983) 'The Clwyd LEA Distance Learning Project for 'A'-level Sociology and Secondary Schools', *British Journal Of Educational Technology* 14 (2), 151–4.

Lewis, R (1995) 'Open and distance learning in Europe: add-on or mainstream?', *Open Learning* (November), 52–6.

Littlefield, D (1994) 'Open learning by PC or paper?', *Personnel Management*, September 1994, 55–8.

Lockwood, F (1992) *Activities in Self-Instructional Texts*, Kogan Page, London.

Mabey, C and Iles, P (1994) 'Introduction', in C Mabey and P Iles, *Managing Learning*, Routledge, London.

Magee, S R and Alexander, D J (1986) 'Training and educating in continuing education', *International Journal of Lifelong Learning* 5 (3), 173–85.

McCollum, A and Calder, J (1995) *Learning Effectiveness of Open and Flexible Learning in Vocational Education: A Literature Review and Annotated Bibliography*, Research Series No. 5, Department for Education and Employment, Sheffield.

Meikle, J and Major, L E (1997) 'Dearing's new deal', *The Guardian*, London.

Merrick, N (1997) 'Colleges keen to be investors in people', *TES*, London.

Merson, M (1995) 'Political explanations for economic decline in Britain and their relationship to policies for education and training', *Journal of Education Policy* 10 (3), 303–15.

Milne, S and Michie, J (1997) 'Blindness of the one-eyed contract king', *The Guardian*, London.

Moore, M (1990) 'Introduction: background and overview of contemporary American distance education', in M Moore, *Contemporary Issues in American Distance Education*, Pergamon Press, Oxford.

Moore, M and Thompson, M (1990) *The Effects of Distance Learning: a Summary of the Literature*, Pennsylvania State University, PA, American Centre of the Study of Distance Education, College of Education.

Morgan, A (1995) 'North Devon College',in J Calder, A McCollum, A Morgan and M Thorpe, *Learning Effectiveness of Open and Flexible Learning in Vocational Education*, Department for Education and Employment, Sheffield, no 58.

Moss, D (1991) 'School pupils' reactions to flexible learning', *British Journal of Educational Technology* 22 (3), 28–38.

Nash, I (1997a) 'Industry university deadline', *TES*, London.

Nash, I (1997b) 'Vauxhall chief's drive on standards', *TES*, London.

National Board of Employment (1992) *Changing Patterns of Teaching and Learning: The Use and Potential of Distance Education Materials and Methods in Australian Higher Education*, Australian Government Publishing Services, Canberra.

Nipper, S (1989) 'Third generation distance learning and computer conferencing', in R Mason and A Kaye, *Mindweave: Communication, Computers and Distance Education*, Pergamon, Oxford.

National Opinion Polls (1992) *Employer Flexible Access: Awareness and Use of Open Learning in Britain*, Department of Employment, Learning Methods Branch, London.

Paine, N (ed)(1988) *Open Learning in Transition: An Agenda for Action*, Kogan Page, London.

Pask, G (1988) 'Learning strategies, teaching strategies, and conceptual or learning style', in R R Schmeck, *Learning Strategies and Learning Styles*, Plenum Press, New York.

Pratt, D (1988) 'Andragogy as a relational concept', *Adult Education Quarterly* 38 (3), 160–81.

Raggatt, P (1993) 'A Society of Opportunity', in J Calder, *Disaffection and Diversity. Overcoming Barriers for Adult Learners*, Falmer Press, London.

Richardson, J T E (1994) 'Cultural specificity of approaches to studying in Higher Education: a literature survey', *Higher Education* 21, 449–68.

Robinson, K (ed)(1989) *Open and Distance Education for Nurses*, Longman, Harlow.

Rumble, G (1997) *The Costs and Economics of Open and Distance Learning*, Kogan Page, London.

Saggers, R (1994) 'Training climbs the corporate agenda', *Personnel Management*, July 1994, 40–45.

Sakamoto, T (1996) 'Innovation in Higher Education and use of (scs) space collaboration system', in *Innovations in Distance and Open Learning*, AAOU 10th Annual Conference, Tehran.

Scriven, B (1991) 'Distance education and open learning – implications for professional development and retraining', *Distance Education* 12 (2), 297–305.

Sloman, M (1994) 'Coming in from the cold: a new role for trainers', *Personnel Management*, January 1994, 24–7.

Snower, D (1997) 'Three diseases that could kill the Welfare to Work initiative', *The Guardian*, London.

Spencer, B (1991) 'Distance education in british trade unions: some preliminary results', *Research in Distance Education* 3 (1), 6–8.

Storey, D J (1994) *Understanding the Small Business Sector*, International Thomson Business Press, London.

Symons, V (1994) 'Company education – organised to meet customer requirements', *Performance and Instruction* 33 (10), 33–5.

Tait, A (ed) (1992) *Key Issue in Open Learning: An Anthology from the Journal of Open Learning 1986–1992*, Longman, Harlow.

Taylor, J C (1997) *Flexible Learning Systems: Opportunities And Strategies For Staff Development In Industry*, Quality Assurance in Distance and Open Learning, 11th AAOU Conference, Institut Teknologi Mara, Kuala Lumpur.

Temple, H (1990) 'Out of the open learning ghetto', in B Farmer, D Eascott and B Lantz, *Making Open Learning Systems Work*, Kogan Page, London.

Temple, H (1991) *Open learning in Industry*, Longman Group UK Ltd, Harlow, Essex.

The Tavistock Institute of Human Relations (1987) *The Open Tech Programme Development Review*, The Tavistock Institute of Human Relations, London.

Thomson, A (1997) 'Colleges too broke to educate properly', *The Times Higher Education Supplement*, London.

Thomson, A (1997) 'Union ponders strike action', *Times Higher Education Supplement*, London.

Tight, M (1995) 'Education, work and adult life: a literature review', *Research Papers in Education* 10 (3), 383–400.

Tight, M (1996) *Key Concepts in Adult Education and Training*, Routledge, London.

Toffler, A (1970) *Future Shock*, Pan Books Ltd, London.

Tough, A (1979) *The Adult's Learning Projects*, Institute for Studies in Education, Toronto; Ontario.

Tuckett, A (1991) *Towards a Learning Workforce*, NIACE, Leicester.

Tuijnman, A C (1992) 'The expansion of adult education and training in Europe; Trends and Issues', *International Review of Education* 38 (6), 673–92.

Vidal, J (1997) 'The real politics of power', *The Guardian*, London.

Warren, J (1994) 'Designing for flexible learning', in R Hoey, *Designing for Learning*, Kogan Page, London.

Wheeler, D and Sillanpaa, M (1997) *The Stakeholder Corporation*, Pitman Publishing, London.

Willmot, M and McLean, M (1994) 'Evaluating Flexible Learning: A Case Study', *Journal for Higher Education* 18 (3), 99–108.

Woodcock, C (1991) 'Where have all the new jobs gone?', *The Guardian*, London.

Woodley, A (1993) 'Disaffection and distance education', in J Calder, *Disaffection and Diversity: Overcoming Barriers for Adult Learners*, The Falmer Press, London.

Wylie, I (1997) 'Working week', *The Guardian*, London.

Index

ABACUS 79
Abbey National 49
access 7, 13
accessibility of training job insecurity 6
accrediting agencies and awards bodies 20
activities 14
admissions
    counselling 38
    policies 54
adults
    education 3, 5, 35
    training 28
Agency staff 63
Allied Maples 58
alternative modes of delivery 11–12
andragogy 101
annual figures 18
aptitude tests 63
Argo Wiggins 21
armed forces 17
assessment 75–85
    centres 26
    work-based 25
assessors, accredited 97
Associated Electrical Engineers Union (AEEU) 21
AT & T 22
attendance, compulsory 64
attrition 53
audio teleconferencing 11–12, 17

B&Q 58
basic skills 42
BBC 21
behaviour changes 88
best practice 9
Boeing 18
bought-in materials 48
BP (British Petroleum) 64
British
    Association of Open Learning (BAOL) 133
    Film Institute 21
    Gas North Western 49
    Steel 89
    Telecom 69
broadcasting 17
BTecs 35
Burton Group 58

capital, organization of 2
careers
    opportunities 7
    prospects 24
CBI 25
certifications 43
child-care problems 54
Citizen Group of Newspapers 49
Civil Service 27
classroom failure 10
Cleveland Open Learning Unit 64
common standards 76
Commonwealth of Learning 2
communications, two-way 11–12
companies
    needs 11
    training needs 10
    training practices 13
competencies
    minimum level of 44
    practical 44
    standards of 44
competency-based
    training 76
    training programmes 42
competition 37, 57
competitive tendering 25–6
compulsory attendance 64
computer-aided instruction 68
computer-based training (CBT) 14, 46
computers
    conferencing 11–12
    mediated communication (CMC) 70
Confederation of British Industry 4
contingency theory 131–2
continuous
    assessment 76
    training 5
contracts
    allocation of 25
    culture 129
control of courses 62
conventional education 3
Coopers and Lybrand 48
core
    skills 42
    stakeholders 20–21
corporate customers 64

correspondence teaching   11–12
costs
   advantages   47
   face-to-face teaching   46
   reductions   57
   savings   46
   structures   11–12
counselling   24, 38, 117
courses
   choice   52
   content   10
   contents   113–15
   study mode   52
   timings   10
   tutors   112
Cresson, Edith   22
curriculum   62
customers
   corporate   64
   requirements   65
cutbacks   128

day-release   47, 117
Dearing report   24
deep approaches   99
definitions   11
Delco Electronics   48, 49
delivery
   costs   11–12
   of learning   10
demand for education   41
deregulation   28
development costs   11–12
didactic teaching   118
disadvantaged learners   39
disaffected adults   38
distance
   education   3, 11–12
   learning, unsupported   108
downsizing   30, 128–9
duration of courses   62, 74
dynamic competition   57

economic decline   23
economically inactive   36
economies of scale   11–2
education
   attainment   35
   goals   7
   and training needs   1
   vocational education courses   74
Education and Science, Department of   28
electronic information technologies   12
employees   7
employer-led vocational education   28
employers
   costs   46
   responsibility for training   27
   sanctions   117
   support   117
employment
   security   7
   training   29

Employment Department, Training, Employment
   and Enterprise Directorate   28
Employment Gazette   10–11
ethnic minorities   36
European
   funded programmes   23
   open universities   17
   training   3
European Commission   125
European Free Trade Association (EFTA)   6
evaluation   118
exams   76
exclusive roles   53
experiential techniques   101
external qualifications   56–7
face-to-face
   provision   12
   support   71
   teaching costs   46
feedbacks   91, 94–5
flexible
   contracts   58
   learning   11
   organizations   58
   training   6
flexistudy   16, 79
Ford Motor Co.   6
Fordist methods of production   58
formal
   assessment procedures   76
   education and training   35
   learning   8
   training   35
formative assessment   76
France   4
full-time education   35
funding   5, 23, 57
Funding Council, FE Colleges   57
Further Education (FE)   16, 18, 29
   Colleges   17–18, 57
   Funding Council (FEFC)   23, 57
   sector   17
Further and Higher Education Act (1992)   26

GCSE   28, 80
General Motors   18
generic
   skills   54
   training   107
Germany   4
Glaxo   57
global companies   124
globalization   2–3, 22
Gothenburg group   99
government
   funded programmes   23
   policy   24
   schemes   36
   training initiatives   3
   training programmes   26
   voluntarist training schemes   4
   White Papers   24
groups

activities 66
Gothenburg group 99
learning 66
stakeholder 19
Store-house Group 58
target 25
work 11, 35
guidance and counselling 24

hierarchical organizations 58
high-end production 47
higher education 21
holist approach 100
home-based
settings 66
study 61, 66
Horticultural Correspondence College 16
House of Commons, Trade and Industry
Committee 4
House of Lords, Select Committee on training 4
Hull College of FE 16, 75
human capital 40–42
general 41
specific 41
human resource capabilities 7

IBM 18, 41
ICDL 67
in-house
production 47
training 17, 48
in-text questions 68
incentives 117
inclusive approach 43
independent
learning packages 14
study 11
individual
learning programmes 26
needs 61
induction training 55, 128
inductions 54
Industrial Training Board (ITB) 16
inequality of opportunity 53
informal
learning 8
training 126
information
about training 53
poor-quality 54
processing 101
society 22
initiative fatigue 37
initiatives 3, 28–9
government training 3
key training 29
leading-edge 9
Inland Revenue 14, 46
Institute of Directors 4
Institute of Personnel and Development 37
Institute of Personnel Management (IPM) 73
instruction, computer-aided 68
instructional

design 11
media 69
interactive videos 49
International
Centre for Distance Education (ICDL) 133
competitiveness 40
Council for Distance Education 22
knowledge systems 2
introduction courses 55
Investors in People Initiative 3

Japan 22
job-related training 18, 35
Jobcentres 54
advisers 133
jobs
flexibility 7
future needs 50
requirements 56

key training initiatives 29
Kingfisher 58
Kodak 18

Land Rover, UK 49
leading-edge initiatives 9
learner-centredness 13
learners
autonomy 13
centred work 11
choice 13
needs 10
study skills 58–9
learning
contracts 119
definition of 18
dependency 84
effectiveness 87, 92
efforts 38
options 15
organizations 15, 44
outcomes 2, 10
process 100–101
requirements 5
skills 82
styles 101
theory 85
levels of
provision 3
training 6
Library and Information Commission 21
lifelong learning 117
line managers, involvement 6
local
authorities 27
education authorities 32
projects 24
training needs 26
location of study 60
long-term unemployed 129
low-end development 47

machine skills 114

management
and supervisory, skills   89
training   4, 7, 69
Manpower Services Commission (MSC)   27
market-based education   37
marketplaces   5
markets
approach to training   110
forces model   5
moving   45
responsiveness   63–4
mass volume   108
Mathieson's Bakers, UK   49
media   12
instructional   69
interactive   68
multiple   62
passive   62
print-based   68
medium-end development   47
mentor support   72
mentoring schemes   65
micro enterprises   125
Microsoft   57
minimum standards   3–4
MOD (Ministry of Defence)   65
Modern Apprenticeships   29
modular courses   76
modularization   11
monitoring   95, 112
motivation   8
Motorola   18, 27
moving markets   45
multi skills   14
workforce   3, 7, 131
multiple stakeholders   92–3

national
Council for Educational Technologies   23
Council for Vocational Qualifications   25
Curriculum   28
Education and Training Targets (NETTS)   3
Extension College   15
Home Study Council   17
Information and Learning Technologies   23
Institute of Adult and Continuing Education   4
Institute of Multimedia Education (NIME)   22
Opinion Polls (NOP)   8
standards   55
Targets for Education and training   25
Technological University (NTU)   17
University Teleconferencing Network (NUTN)   17
NEC   67
Technician Training Scheme   79
Nissan UK   9
Non-Advanced Further Education Initiative (NAFE)   29
non-formal learning   8
non-statutory training organizations   24
NOP (National Opinion Polls   8
North America, joint programmes   7
North Devon College   75

NVQs   3
system of assessment   77

occupational
competencies   25
levels   18
off-the-job training   126
off-the-shelf materials   47
older workers   36
one-way video/two-way audio programmes   17
open
access   7, 63
Colleges   21, 25
learning   11, 13–14
centres   25
implementation   14–5
packs   49
policy   9
practice   9
programmes   7, 9
provision   8
workbooks   45
pedagogy   7
Tech Programme   7, 25
Tech Unit (OTU)   24
University   15–16
opportunities
costs   44
inequality of   53
organization and management of training   4
outputs   92
outside suppliers   30
outsourcing   30, 128–9
over-training   45
overlapping terminology   11

pacing   74–5
paid leave   3
part-time
students   34
studies   35
participation, barriers to   13
performance
indicators   89–91
measures   57
students   76
work   118
person skills   114
personal development   109
Personal Investment Authority (PIAS)   43
PICKUP   28
pilot schemes   129
Plymouth College of Further Education   16, 64, 73
Post Office   14, 31, 77
Counters Ltd   45
post-Fordist
patterns of production and organization   5
principles   2
post-school
education   34
participation   35
preparatory work   82
prerequisites   61

price competition   57
print-based media   68
prior learning   38, 117
   accreditation   11
private training providers   16, 34
privatisations   128
process volume   109
production costs   12
productivity   10
programmed learning   69
public
   education   5
   exams   76
Public Accounts Committee   26
Public Service Satellite Consortium   17
publishers   20

qualifications   18, 56–7
quality of learning   122
questionnaires   97

Rank Xerox   14, 18
records of specified competencies   76
regulatory
   bodies   34
   practices   43
residential
   settings   66
   weekends   49
reskilling   45
response rates   97
Reuters   59
roll-on roll-off courses   60
Rover Motor Company   6
running costs   46

Safeway   14, 41, 73
sales staff, training   7
satellites   17–18
Scholl   16
Scottish and Universal   49
selection for participation   63
self study courses   61
self-confidence   103
self-directed learners   37–9
self-directed learning   18, 37–8
self-employed   36
self-paced courses   61
self-paces   116
self-renewing organizations   30
self-study packages   119
self-training   127
serialist learners   100
Severn Trent Water   44
short courses   50
Shropshire Health Authority   49
simulations   66
skills   42
   generic   54
   learner study   58–9
   learning   39
   machine   114
   management and supervisory   89

person   114
shortages   8, 24
technical   56
training   88
small
   businesses   24, 125
   and medium enterprises (SME)   3, 124–5
   volume   108
Sony   57
Space Collaboration System (SCS)   22
specialisation   14
staff
   agency   63
   appraisals   55
   development   11
   motivation   47–8
   profiles   58
   training and development   7, 11
stakeholder alliances   19
stakeholders
   existing   26
   groups   19
   multiple   92–3
   new   21–3, 26
   perspective   19–21
   policy   58
standards
   assessment and verification   76
   comparability   76
static competition   57
Store-house Group   58
student-centred courses   62
students
   numbers   34
   part-time   34
   performance   76
study settings   65–6
success
   measure of   57
   perceptions of   20
suitability for training   56
summative assessment   76
supervised training   7, 38
supervision   117
supply-side models   53
support   62
surface approaches   99
surveys   98

target groups   25
targeted provision   39
Tavistock Institute of Human Relations   25
Teachers into Business and Industry   28
technical
   skills   56
   training   69
Technical and Vocational Education Initiative
      (TVE)   28
technology
   appropriate   68
   electronic information   12
   new   12
telecommunications   17

telematics   22
telephone support   70
temporary work   129
Tesco   9, 41
third party delivery   25
Thistle Hotels   49
time limits   61
time:ables   121
Trade and Industry, Department of (DTI)   28, 125
trainees   45
trainers   10, 45
training
    agency   28
    attachment   66
    bodies   4
    budgets   64
    Commission   28
    consultants   32
    costs   32
    courses   50
    departments   31
        reorganization   30
    effectiveness   91
    and Enterprise Councils (TECS)   16, 25, 126
    instructors   31
    leave   4
    levies   4
    managers   112
    needs   9, 58, 106
    officers   31
    operatives   7
    options   106
    packages   32
    practice   14
    premises   62, 65
    programmes   2, 14
        tailored   10
    provision   106
        quality   56
    responsibility for   6
    sites   2
    solutions   39
    standards   26
    Standards Council   26
    strategies   16
    trends   7
    videos   42
Triplex Safety Glass   49
trust   128
TSB   44

TUC   6
tuition fees   41
tutor-led provision   14
tutorials   121
    in print   68
tutors
    options   71
    roles   70
    support   121

underpinning knowledge   44
Understanding British Industry (UBI)   28
unemployed   25
    long-term   129
    participants   36
unemployment rates   37
Unison, Open College   21
unit costs   47–8
universities   32
University of Wisonsin   12
updating   45, 54

value added concept   57
video, conferencing   12, 17
videos   14
visual aids   14
vocational
    education   25, 28
        courses, duration   74
        employer-led   28
        and training, practical   1
    qualifications   25
voluntary organizations   25

Woolworths   58
work
    performance   118
    placements   66
    schedules   47
work-based
    activities   112
    assessment   25
    learning   5
    training   2
work-related training   10
workforces
    flexible   2
    multi skilled   3, 7, 131
World Bank   131
written materials   18